Restoring
Furniture

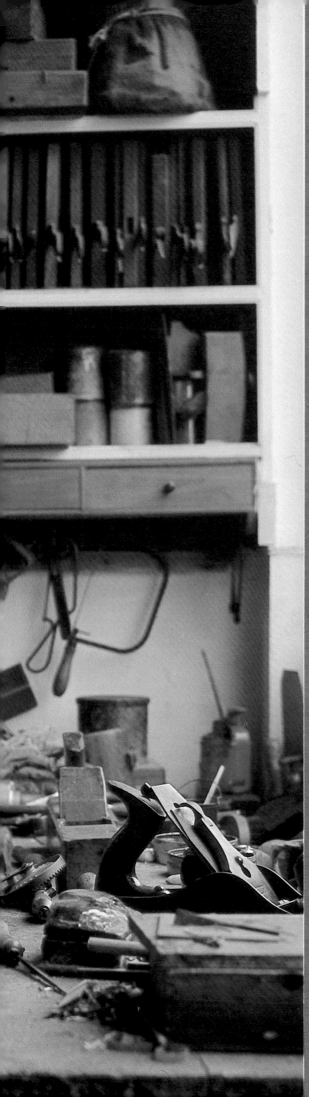

Restoring Furniture

Kenneth Davis
and Thom Henvey

Macdonald Orbis

A *Macdonald Orbis* BOOK

© Orbis Publishing Ltd, London 1978
© Macdonald & Co (Publishers) Ltd, London 1988

First published in paperback in Great Britain in 1984
by Orbis Publishing Ltd

Reprinted in Great Britain in 1988
by Macdonald & Co (Publishers) Ltd
London & Sydney

a member of Maxwell Pergamon Publishing Corporation plc

Printed in Italy by O.F.S.A., Milan

ISBN: 0-356-17548-0

Macdonald & Co (Publishers) Ltd
Greater London House
Hampstead Road
London
NW1 7QX

The publishers would like to acknowledge the help of the
following in permitting the use of photographs shown on the
pages listed.

6: Nordiska Museet, Stockholm
11: Abbey Road Antiques
16-17: The Building Research Establishment, Bucks
10: Rijksmuseum, Amsterdam
22: The American Museum in Britain, Bath
27: Deirdre Serssin
33: Tubby/Elizabeth Whiting

Studio photography: Peter Pugh-Cook
Illustrations: David Parr
Advisory editor: Angela Jeffs
Canework: Sarah Williamson
Upholstery: Lindsay Vernon
Designer: Ingrid Mason

Contents

The Amateur Restorer

Indispensable professional advice on how to date and assess your old furniture, and the properties and advantages of different woods

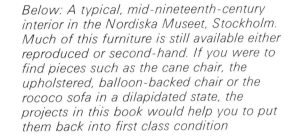

Below: A typical, mid-nineteenth-century interior in the Nordiska Museet, Stockholm. Much of this furniture is still available either reproduced or second-hand. If you were to find pieces such as the cane chair, the upholstered, balloon-backed chair or the rococo sofa in a dilapidated state, the projects in this book would help you to put them back into first class condition

Few workshop satisfactions equal those of restoring the beauty of old furniture, so often buried under layers of varnish and paint, covered with dust and oil stains or split and broken. The skilled replacement of damaged legs or mouldings, the renewal of hinges or inlay and the final finishing and polishing produce a period piece which is a joy not only to the craftsman but also to his or her family.

Furniture, both old and new, is becoming increasingly expensive. Wood commands high prices, so furniture is costly to build. And much modern furniture is designed under the eye of the production manager rather than the craftsman so that in a short period of time the consumer is forced to refurnish his or her home, again with inferior furniture. On the other hand, solid and attractive pieces are readily available in dilapidated condition and while rare antiques are bought by dealers and restored for resale at inflated prices, nineteenth- and early twentieth-century pieces or traditional country furniture can still be purchased at reasonable and often minimal cost.

With a willingness to learn the basic techniques of restoration—often surprisingly simple and requiring only straightforward materials and know-how—the amateur can easily transform seemingly ugly and repainted items into fresh and sturdy pieces of furniture. Often fairly modern pieces are in period style and only need knowledgeable rebuilding to restore them to the fine copies they are. Later, with the confidence gained tackling uncomplicated pieces, the amateur can gradually progress to work with more challenging and valuable antiques.

The possibilities will be demonstrated through the craftsmanship of Kenneth Davis, one of Britain's leading antique furniture restorers. He has rejuvenated furniture of all ages and styles and has the craftsman's eye and sensitivity together with an understanding of the processes that can be used by the layman in the restoration of pieces not fragile enough to warrant expensive, specialist treatment. His work is unsigned, and can be found in stately homes and famous historical buildings, seemingly untouched for centuries, a testimony not only to his learned craftsmanship but also to the delicacy and deftness of his approach and technique.

Furniture restoration is a relatively new craft. In the 1920s, after the upsurge and instability of World War I, collecting period furniture became fashionable and antique shops were crammed with the contents of country houses in Britain, Europe and America. Antique shops and auction rooms abounded with four-poster Victorian beds, Elizabethan oak chairs and seventeenth-century chests. But as the number of collectors increased, so did the demand for craftsmen who specialized in restoration. Many of these craftsmen, including Kenneth Davis, who have spent their lives rescuing antique furniture from decay, began their careers during this period.

Kenneth Davis displays all the skills of the furniture restorer. He is not only a master craftsman but he also has a keen knowledge of the history of styles and the use of wood throughout the centuries. In the various sections of this book he shares his special knowledge, suggesting how the amateur can furnish his or her home with durable, quality period furniture.

No special tools are needed for furniture restoration other than those of the ordinary carpenter. One or two new tools may be needed for repairing upholstery but they are inexpensive and, if you buy good quality, will last a lifetime.

The skills and methods examined here can be applied to almost all period furniture, whether it is a nineteenth-century chest of drawers or the more common Welsh oak dresser. A series of projects, photographed and described at each stage of the restoration, will show the techniques in their practical context. These projects have been chosen to demonstrate the full range of skills, from simple cleaning to total rebuilding.

A guide on how to buy old furniture is also included. This explains the faults to watch for, how to date pieces, recognize woods and veneers and how to tell if some restoration work—altering the style of the piece, for instance—has already been done. This will enable amateurs to make a quick evaluation of a piece of furniture seen in a second hand store or auction room. With this knowledge, you can furnish your home with taste and personality.

This book is intended for those who wish to learn the basics of restoration and those who are beginning to study furniture in more detail. The majority of repairs that confront the amateur restorer are simply a matter of following instructions. The furniture chosen for the projects was selected for its practicality in the modern home, as well as for attractiveness. It was also chosen to display the skills which apply to the restoration of a chest of drawers as well as to a writing bureau. The projects demonstrate how to remake joints, the best way to restore inlay, fittings and panels, the skills of mixing stains and polishes, the best ways to prepare decorative parts such as legs, cornices or brackets, and how to find and use

fabrics to their best effect in upholstering chairs, chaises longues and settees. One project shows the way to restore a simple piece of cane furniture.

After completing one or two pieces, an amateur restorer will have gained the experience, natural deftness and confidence necessary to tackle more ambitious projects. The different projects are graded so that the pieces which require the more knowledgeable kind of workmanship come last. It is also to be hoped that as the beginner completes projects, the need for fuller knowledge about the history of furniture, wood and the styles of the cabinet-makers will become apparent. To track down elusive pieces, to date them to within a decade or so and then to repair and refinish them are all enjoyable and economic exercices.

Finding furniture

Furniture restoration is becoming increasingly popular, and there is a corresponding growth in the number of dealers. These range from the

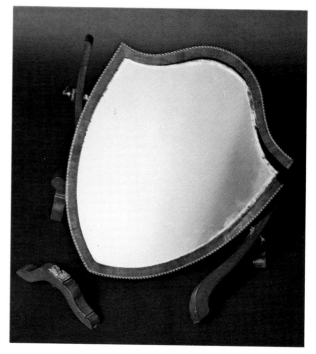

renowned auction houses in the major cities to the local second-hand merchant.

Rare antique furniture is obviously too expensive for all except the professional buyers, specialists and private collectors. But there are a large number of auction rooms and old furniture shops where inexpensive originals and good quality reproduction pieces can be found. There are also many second-hand stores where the amateur collector can keep an eager eye open for the attractive bargains that occasionally crop up.

Auction rooms tend to provide a wide variety of old and new furniture at the cheapest prices since they are often essentially wholesalers. Through regular attendance at auctions you can learn how

to handle pieces, and listen to dealers' evaluations before attempting to bid. In this way you will gradually build up a fund of knowledge so that if you found it difficult at first to distinguish between mahogany and walnut, you will quickly learn not only to do that, but also how to differentiate rosewood inlay from tulipwood inlay. You will also learn the approximate prices of particular periods and styles and so will be able to pitch your bids without losing money.

This kind of knowledge will help a great deal when buying privately. Not only will you be able to date and evaluate a piece, but you will also be able to make an educated guess as to its mark-up price so that you can negotiate confidently.

Above left: With a few simple restoration techniques, a broken mahogany mirror can look as good as new (above). The joints were all strengthened and new mirror fittings were added. The whole piece was then revived and repolished to bring the wood back to its original brilliance

The amateur restorer

Second-hand stores tend to be furniture grave-yards and most of their furniture may be unsuitable. Nevertheless, they do have occasional bargains and so should not be totally ignored.

It should be stressed that it will be necessary to exercise caution, especially if you intend to invest relatively large sums of money. Some dealers do attempt to pass off reproductions as authentic pieces, and adjust the price accordingly. Establishing whether a piece is genuine can be a problem for some buyers. If a piece is well made, performs its function and is good value for money, it may not matter to you that it is a reproduction. But if you want to buy or unexpectedly find yourself in the position of being able to purchase genuine antiques there are ways to protect yourself. The safest thing is to have the piece checked by an expert. If you cannot afford this or if the price of the piece does not warrant such additional expense, the next best thing is to obtain a concisely written description of the article of furniture from the dealer so that you have a reasonable chance of returning the item for your money if it turns out to be other than the seller claimed.

Dating furniture

Knowing what to look for when buying or dating old furniture is a skill that may take some time to acquire. Much wasted time, effort and cost can be avoided, however, by becoming acquainted with certain basic characteristics of good craftsmanship, knowing a few tips for testing authenticity and some general hints on evaluating its quality.

The term 'period' as used throughout the rest of the chapter applies to all quality-built, as opposed to mass-produced, furniture made prior to World War II. This will exclude furniture made with any kind of plastic, compressed particle board (such as chipboard or hardboard), plywoods or block-boards—sheet materials made from blocks of wood glued together and faced on both sides with a thick veneer. It will also exclude pieces made with mostly African timbers (such as Podo red or white Maranti) and Japanese timber. The furniture will not have pressed or lacquered metal hinges or fittings, rubber shod castor wheels, or wire nails or the more modern screws.

The timber most likely to be used would be a hardwood, such as English or Austrian oak, English or French walnut, sycamore, chestnut, birch, ash, mahogany, beech, teak, western red cedar, pine or rosewood. A good rule of thumb is that the main construction should be made of a hardwood, such as those outlined above, and the inside of drawers or bottoms of chests of any stable, common

Right: There are many places where furniture can be picked up second-hand. It pays to examine the furniture closely. Some shops specialize, as this one does in pine, and the furniture may have been renovated already

The amateur restorer

wood. In short, the parts of the piece of furniture in direct contact with room temperature will be made of hardwood.

Hardwood was used for quality furniture because of movement—expansion on cold days, contraction on hot days. This, together with the fact that wood is strongest along the grain and weakest across the grain, dictates the methods of construction of furniture if it is to be at all durable.

One of the most important things to look for is that the grain of any boards which are adjacent or at right angles runs in the same direction. If this is not so the resulting stress of contraction and expansion will eventually cause the wood to split. The larger surfaces of cabinets, wardrobes, chests, and clocks were usually made of several planks of solid wood to prevent excessive bowing. These planks were planed along their longest edges until they were flat and square. They were then placed together and rubbed against each other until they mated perfectly before being either glued along these edges or held together with tongue-and-groove joints. The grain ran vertically on the backs and sides of such pieces as a further measure against bowing.

However, there is usually some bowing in old furniture because of age and especially since the introduction of central heating in most homes. The outside surfaces on many old pieces will be slightly bowed and not as flat as when originally constructed. This is because the outside has been subjected to the varieties of room temperature while the inside, being unpolished, has dried out more over the course of time. The resulting shrinkage of the inside of the board will cause a slight contouring of the outside. This shrinkage is always in the width and never along the length of the grain.

This bowing will also occur if a hardwood veneer, such as walnut, was laid on a softwood such as pine, since the pine will have dried out more quickly and the veneer laid across its grain, resists shrinkage. This will particularly apply to Queen Anne furniture and to most early eighteenth-century pieces which immediately followed this period.

The behaviour of wood in old furniture will tell you a great deal about its quality and even its age. More details on this subject will be given in the section on woods and particularly in the section on the basic techniques used in restoration.

The finish is a good indication of the quality and value of a piece of furniture. The most likely finishes on old pieces of furniture are linseed oil for teak, beeswax and turpentine, lime bleach or fuming for oak and a shellac-based polish for mahogany, walnut and most other hardwoods.

The object of French or shellac-based polishing is to first make the surface as flat and smooth as possible and then to apply a coat of polish, rubbing it back to the wood to fill any crevices. Several coats used to be needed for a perfect finish, but with modern French polishes just one can often be sufficient. This process will bring out the depth

Right: With experience, a knowledge of construction, and historical detail, the amateur restorer can easily assess and identify these seven chairs, all at various stages of repair.
1. An American rocker, Edwardian, in walnut
2. A round back Victorian bedroom chair in birch
3. A Victorian country bentwood chair in birch
4. A Regency bamboo chair
5. A bentwood chair, dated about 1860
6. A Victorian upholstered chair in walnut
7. A Windsor chair, 1780.

and iridescence of the grain, and the resultant lustrous sheen is known as the patina. This is the surface of the polish and years of repolishing will continue to enhance its depth.

By studying the patina carefully you should be able to estimate if the piece is genuinely old. A surface with a good patina should have an almost translucent, mellow tone and will usually be a little darker than the original colour of the wood. There are, as was mentioned, a number of liquids on the market today which, if used skilfully, can result in fairly convincing imitations of genuine French polishing, but the genuine French polished piece will have a mellow feeling while the modern substitute will usually be very shiny.

The veneer on a piece can also reveal a great deal. A veneer is a thin piece of wood which was cut by hand until the early nineteenth century. Veneers were traditionally used to enable decorative but unstable woods to be used in conjunction with stable but dull structural woods. And it was the use of veneering that subsequently made marquetry and inlay possible. Damage to veneers can easily be repaired. But if the whole surface is beginning to rise this can prove difficult to repair.

On the best furniture, mouldings and decorations are scribed or carved into the solid panels. They will not be pinned. If they are applied they will either be glued or jointed. Many inlays were added at a later date to period furniture to give it a look of authenticity and should be scrutinized.

On better quality furniture, fittings and hinges were made in brass or bronze; they were either handcut or cast and sometimes even soldered with silver. Their colour will have dulled and on very old pieces, unless the previous owners were obsessive, they will more than likely be scratched. If the piece is fairly inexpensive, you can ask for one of the fittings to be taken off so that you can see what the wood looks like underneath. The colour should look different and slightly newer, certainly not identical. There are likely to be rust marks where the metal has discoloured the wood.

These are most of the things you should look for to determine if a piece is old and of good

The amateur restorer

Left: Scratching with a coin on a hidden part of a heavily varnished piece will reveal the original wood

Below: Woodworm is a major problem, small holes can be easily filled but more seriously affected areas need to be completely replaced

Right: This fine mahogany hinged table has badly warped. Usually due to damp or too much heat, it is a major repair and should not be attempted

Finding faults

There are various obvious points to bear in mind when examining old furniture. Many faults, either due to botched restoration or because of the ravages of nature, come about through neglect or ignorance. Warping is a common fault, usually caused by exposure to unequal temperatures, such as when a table is placed against a radiator. This will bring about great strains in the wood, especially if the conditions are severe. Warping is perhaps most common in tables because the top is initially well polished, and frequently repolished, while the bottom is often left bare.

Examples of botched restoration are usually obvious, except where a dealer has done a superficial job to fool the inexpert. Watch out for oriental lacquer work, particularly red japanned work, which is usually black, heavily lacquered and resembles an egg-shell.

Stains, such as ink, wine marks and water crescents are other faults to watch for. These are not so serious and can usually be dealt with by rubbing down the spoiled area and then waxing. If the stain is more obstinate, use one of the other methods outlined later in this book.

Years of wear and tear on a piece of furniture can add a certain charm but some bruises may have defaced the wood. If they are not too deep they can be repaired although a slight scar may still be left. If there are deep gouges they may be beyond any kind of action.

Pests and diseases such as beetles or fungus are often ignored by people buying old furniture. Damage caused by the furniture beetle and woodworm is easy to recognize. Various products are on the market for dealing with these problems but if the damage has gone very far you may have to remove a foot, a bracket or a piece of moulding and replace it. This will involve many techniques discussed in the projects in this book.

Wood

An understanding of wood, both old and new, is essential for the amateur restorer. It is simply not enough to know about styles and periods. It is

quality. Of course there are further points specifically related to the age and period of particular pieces, but this kind of detail will usually only apply if the piece is fairly rare.

There are also more esoteric differences on which to base your assessment of a piece, according to the tools used and the presence of any nails or screws. Before the eighteenth century, for example, wood was cut with straight saws. In the nineteenth century circular saws were introduced because they could cut faster, but they left distinct ridges around the cut which can be felt with the finger. Until the 1800s nails were hand-cut prior to being machine-pressed. Wooden screws were not tapered until the nineteenth century and the threads were handfiled into a shallow spiral. One test of authenticity in furniture in which nails have been used is staining in the wood caused by oxidation.

Many of these points will not apply to what has come to be known as country furniture, such as Welsh dressers and pieces from nineteenth-century American ranches. The wood used in antique furniture will usually be hard and heavy while country-made pieces will be heavier in construction but lighter, in woods with more porous grains. Much country furniture is extremely well made and has a charm and beauty within reach of the pockets of most collectors. The restoration of such pieces should be done with as much care as is given to a rarer antique.

imperative for the restorer to be able to identify the more common woods and to understand how they react so that he or she will be able to match old and new wood easily.

Every species of tree produces a different fine structure of cells making up its wood. This results in distinctive surface patterns, colours and lustres, plus qualities of texture, weight and hardness which can be readily recognized once you have had a little experience.

Woods are usually divided into softwoods and hardwoods. This division does not relate to hardness in any literal sense. Some softwoods are harder than hardwoods and *vice versa*. Balsa wood, for example, is a hardwood. The term softwood does not refer to lightness in weight or colour or imply weakness. It refers to woods from the family of coniferous (cone bearing) trees which are porous and moisture bearing. Pine is the best-known softwood. Generally, softwoods are strong and used in the unseen parts of quality furniture, drawers, for example.

Hardwoods derive from the broadleaved family of trees and include the oaks, teaks, birches and mahoganies. Hardwoods are used by cabinet-makers because of their hardness and good appearance, hence their survival and value in older antique pieces.

After trees are felled, timber is cut and seasoned. Seasoning is a controlled removal of moisture, and may be done naturally or in a kiln under controlled conditions. Generally, modern wood is not of the same quality as that used in the past. In the eighteenth century, one generation of craftsmen started the seasoning of timber for the succeeding generation to use. The timber was cut into long planks, stacked carefully under cover and allowed to dry out very slowly for up to 50 years, expanding and contracting to natural atmospheric conditions until it reached an ideal dryness for use. The internal stresses of kiln dried wood tend to result in warping and other defects because the moisture is extracted too quickly. One of the problems of restoration is finding a naturally seasoned wood if part of an old piece of furniture requires replacement, and knowing what to do should you have to match a modern mahogany with an older piece.

There is another problem in matching woods besides that of seasoning. The depth of colour of wood increases with age. A modern piece of oak is an off-white yellow while the oak used for Elizabethan furniture has mellowed to a deep rich brown. The amateur restorer may not encounter such extreme examples, but if he or she works with mahogany of most ages, the same problem will have to be overcome.

Each wood has its own peculiarities. In early walnut veneers there is always a depth of mellow faded colour which is difficult to copy or match. Queen Anne furniture, for example, made from walnut veneers, is difficult to restore because of colour matching.

European Beech (hardwood)
Beech is a sturdy wood which is used extensively for all furniture, particularly for the solid parts in cabinet work and chairs. European beech is very enduring and stains and polishes well. One disadvantage is its tendency to shrink

Indian Rosewood (hardwood)
For more than two centuries Indian rosewood has been prized for fine cabinet work and inlay. Indian rosewood is plainer than other varieties of rosewood which usually come from Brazil. Rosewood veneers were popular in eighteenth-century England

European Oak (hardwood)
Traditionally the structural wood of legendary durability, European oak is used for all quality restoration work. It needs care when nailing and screwing, but stains, polishes and glues well. Oak is liable to corrode if in contact with metal

Sycamore (Maple in the U.S.) (hardwood)
This is a light-coloured wood with a very fine texture. It has an irregular grain and stains and polishes well. It is suitable for turned and cabinet work and is the traditional wood for the backs of violins

British Honduras Mahogany (hardwood)
From 1760 onwards this was the basic wood for quality furniture such as dining tables and cabinets. Today it is expensive but since it finishes so beautifully it is ideal for small dimensional work and it does not shrink or distort

European Birch (hardwood)
This is a very strong wood with an exceptional ability to hold tacks. In the nineteenth century it was used for wardrobes because it gave an interesting 'silky' finish. Today it is used for upholstery frames and interior work

Ceylon Ebony (hardwood)
This wood has a straight grain and its uniform black colour can, on rare occasions, be tinged with brown streaks. It is extremely brittle and difficult to glue but it polishes beautifully. Ceylon ebony is used wherever it can be shown to decorative advantage

European Ash (hardwood)
Ash is an outstandingly tough wood but its use for furniture making has always been limited. It is found in turned work, and is sometimes used for framing. It can act as a substitute for oak in some cases. Its best known use is in the making of cricket bats

American Whitewood (hardwood)
This wood was popular in the 1920s and 1930s but in England its use has been restricted to interior joinery and the frames of cabinets and cupboards. It is regarded as a reliable foundation for veneering but is unsuitable for any turned or bent work.

Scots Pine or European Redwood (softwood)
This wood is extensively used in basic joinery and frames and sometimes for veneers. It is not very resistent to decay however, and is regarded as a basic wood to be used where it will not show

Teak (hardwood)
Teak is rarely found in old European furniture although it is fashionable for modern domestic furniture. However old oriental furniture can be constructed with solid teak. In restoration teak can be useful as a show-wood but it tends to split

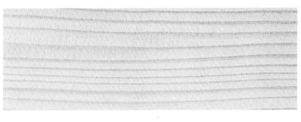

European Spruce (softwood)
This white, wild-grained wood is very tough and easy to sand, glue and nail. It takes a good finish and provides a base for veneering but is not very resistent to decay. European spruce tends to become lighter in colour when exposed to the light

European Walnut (hardwood)
Walnut is an outstanding decorative wood, sometimes with a wavy grain. The wood used for furniture is taken from the base of the tree near the roots. It is therefore very expensive. It polishes and stains superbly and is used in highly figured veneers

Bird's Eye Maple (hardwood)
This is a pale wood, sometimes called rock maple, with an unusual 'bird's eye' figure. It stains, polishes and glues well but is difficult to nail. Bird's eye maple was very popular for decorative veneering in the 1930s

European Cherry (hardwood)
Like other fruitwoods, cherry was used in early provincial furniture, often as a decorative veneer. It is inclined to warp and is therefore used only in small sections but glues and polishes well. It is widely used in America for cabinet and furniture making

Ramin (hardwood)
Ramin will not be found in any antique furniture since it was only introduced in the 1950s. Ramin provides an excellent substitute for beech in carcass construction and framing. It is used in long thin sections, such as the rails of a chaise-longue

The colour of oak, even over a relatively short period, mellows greatly. The older the piece, the more pronounced the change. You will immediately notice the depth of colour in old oak when it is cut to replace a panel, for example. Many of the problems of colour change can be overcome through various bleaching techniques and in the final staining or polishing of the repaired piece of furniture. These will be discussed in the section on polishing on page 30 and in the different projects.

Blending and harmonizing the colours of woods is a skill that can make a vast difference in a job of restoration. It is an area of restoration in which the greatest care is called for. In an old piece of furniture most of the colour is in the wood itself. This is why it is important to remove the polished surface without damaging the colour in the wood so that the wood can once again be polished to resemble its original patina. The beauty of age-coloured wood cannot be restored artifically with the help of modern dyes or bleaches, so any mistakes made in stripping are irrevocable. However, if you are careful, you can polish the carefully stripped surface to a good durable shine which will retain the depth of colour of the original patina.

Besides its use in major structural work, wood has also been used in ways which have become specialized crafts themselves. Such skills are generally beyond the scope of the amateur and are perhaps best left alone. A knowledge of the terms and techniques, however, is useful.

Marquetry is the use of different coloured woods to achieve a decorative effect. It is closely allied to inlay except that in the latter stones like lapis lazuli and agate, or ivory, mother-of-pearl and tortoiseshell are used instead of wood.

Both marquetry and inlay are done by cutting a shallow strip from the surface of a cabinet or table top. The groove is then filled with the coloured stones (inlay) or woods (marquetry). These can be arranged to achieve complex and beautiful patterns which are then polished. The greatest exponent of this kind of work was André Boulle, a Frenchman who lived from 1642 to 1732. The main materials he used were tortoiseshell, pewter and brass. His technique, called Boullework, has been copied through the centuries but it is a difficult craft and so pieces that need restoration should be avoided by the amateur.

Parquetry and intarsia are other forms of wood mosaic. In parquetry, woods of many different colours are inlaid to form geometrical patterns and then smoothed and polished. Intarsia is a similar technique but instead of geometrical shapes, the wood is inlaid to create pictures.

If you wish to try your hand at any of these techniques you could learn a great deal by reproducing a small piece from a furniture catalogue. In this way you will gain valuable experience before trying the technique on decorated and perhaps valuable pieces.

Left: A chipped piece of veneer decorates this tea caddy from the mid-eighteenth century (Sheraton). The base wood is probably oak, with satinwood as the background. The major design is holly (the two central shapes), and the leaves and edging are in ebony and boxwood. By comparison, the detail on the right, from a late eighteenth-century Dutch serving table, is in perfect condition. Again the background is satinwood veneer with ebony and sycamore for the detail

Veneers

Veneering is a skill that can be tackled by any amateur restorer. A veneer is a thin layer of wood, originally cut by hand, but done by machine after the early part of the nineteenth century. Rare, expensive and decorative woods were cut into thin slices and then used to face common, cheaper wood.

Veneer can be successfully applied by hand without specialized equipment such as the heated presses used by professionals. It is advisable to begin by veneering flat surfaces before progressing to deal with curves.

Veneer may be hard to find in shops, and you will certainly have to spend some time looking for the better quality materials. The ideal way is to go to a specialist in veneers but they are usually only found in the larger cities and normally will only sell in large sheets. Some lumber yards stock the more common veneers but can order the exotic types at additional expense. Antique dealers who restore some of their own furniture may be willing to sell some, while an increasing number of art and handicraft shops sell small pieces for marquetry. A number of artificial veneers are on the market and although some of these are of good quality they can never look or feel as good as well-cut natural veneers. Modern veneers are thinner than the old veneers, so you may like to collect old broken pieces of furniture to cut up for materials.

Faults in veneer can range from simple blemishes which are easily corrected, to major repairs such as the replacement of marquetry. One of the most common faults is that of chipped corners and edges, especially near doors and drawers. Because of the continual friction, drawer runners often suffer from chipped veneer.

Fabrics

Many factors contribute to the choice of fabric to finish your upholstery, such as the colour scheme of the room in which it is to serve. The fabric selected should be an upholstery fabric—as strong and hardwearing as you can find and afford.

It should also be closely woven as it will undergo much friction and rubbing. Fabrics with a smooth finish will keep clean longer than those with a pile or nap, such as velvet or cord. Obviously, dark colours are more practical than light ones.

Included in the range of upholstery fabrics are moquette, a wool and cotton mix with a pile, which looks like harsh velvet; tapestry, a stiff fabric with a woven pattern; tweed, a particularly durable fabric; velvet, expensive but the most widely used fabric in upholstering; vinyl, which often looks like leather and is easily cleaned; and hide-leather, which is expensive but very hard wearing.

More traditional fabrics are brocades, damasks, tapestries and woven patterns such as Regency stripes. Alternatively, you could use a piece of crewel embroidery on a linen twill background or a piece of needlepoint on a canvas background.

To calculate the amount needed, measure the overall length and width of the seat and allow an extra all-round six inches (150 mm) so that the fabric can be easily stretched and turned under the seat frame. To calculate for a chaise longue or large sofa, measure the old covering and add six inches all round for the material which has been trimmed. If there is no old cover you will have to measure each rectangular area of the sofa, allowing an added all-round six inches for covering the springs and padding, and another six inches all-round for facility of working. Then total the square area of the separate rectangular pieces.

The Tool Kit

A good selection of tools is essential for any restoration job. This chapter outlines the basic equipment required for the work and the fundamental construction techniques used in the building of furniture

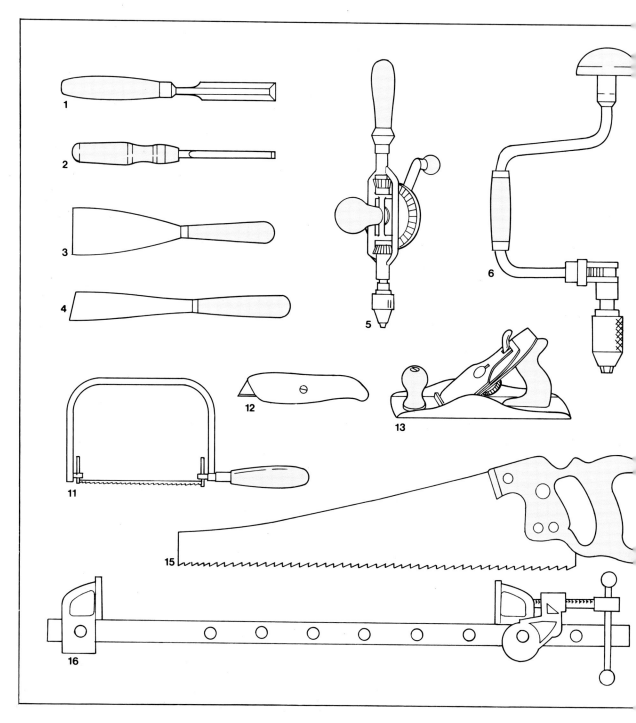

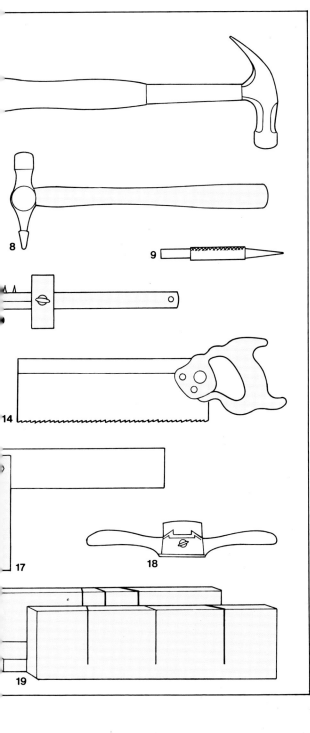

A skeleton tool kit, no bigger than that used for most ordinary do-it-yourself jobs, is all that is necessary for furniture restoration.

It is important that the tools are in good condition and that they are sharp, especially the chisels and planes. These can be sharpened by grinding them on a grindstone, if the edges are damaged, and then fining the edge with an oil-stone. It is often necessary to cut off very thin sections of wood, so it is essential to keep your tools sharp.

If grinding the tools is unnecessary, then all that you need to do is to sharpen them on an oil-stone. These are available in various grades and it is ideal to have both a coarse and a fine oil-stone. The coarser stone is used if the tool is in bad condition after cutting a hard or gritty material, while the fine stone will give that extra tone to a tool which is slightly dulled.

If you wish to have a still finer edge it will be necessary to hone the tools. This can be done on an old piece of leather with an abrasive paste coating in the manner of the old fashioned barber. Honing polishes steel and produces an edge as fine as a razor.

The most important tool to keep sharp is the steel scraper. Scrapers are made in various thicknesses. The very finest can be used for heavy lacquer work while the thicker scrapers can take off very fine shavings from wood, leaving a smooth surface ready for polishing.

Left: Some basic tools are essential to the amateur furniture restorer. A few are illustrated here and others will be shown throughout the special projects section.
1. *Bevel-edged chisel*
2. *Mortise chisel*
3. *Stripping knife*
4. *Filling knife*
5. *Wheel brace*
6. *Swing brace*
7. *Claw hammer*
8. *Cross-pein hammer*
9. *Nail punch*
10. *Gauge*
11. *Coping saw*
12. *Cutting knife*
13. *Metal plane*
14. *Tenon saw*
15. *Panel saw*
16. *Sash clamp*
17. *Try-square*
18. *Spokeshave*
19. *Mitre box*

The tool kit

Below: A pine and curly maple tailoress's counter. This piece of Shaker furniture (1820–23) has a strong, stable construction with few embellishments. It is an example of the basic carcass construction of traditional furniture which is shown in diagrammatic form on the right

Basic Construction

The basis of any cabinet, sideboard, wardrobe, cupboard or bookcase is a carcass or box. This forms the main structure of the piece. A typical cabinet of almost any period will have the top and other major areas constructed from several large planks of wood, planed flat and then glued along their longest edges. If these boards are quite thick they are usually held together with tongue-and-groove joints.

The traditional method of construction is to make the back with one or more panels, the grain running vertically. The sides are constructed in one piece. These panels are then joined together by means of vertical strips of wood about three or four inches (80 mm to 100 mm) wide and three-quarter inch (18 mm) thick, grooved on both edges. The panels fit into these grooves making gluing unnecessary.

The constructed back panels are then fitted into grooves made in the wood on the sides, top and bottom of the piece. The sides themselves are normally constructed from one substantial solid end.

The front of most cabinets usually consists of rails running horizontally and vertically to form frames for the doors or drawers. The front is secured by mortise and tenon joints into the sides. In this kind of joint the end of one member

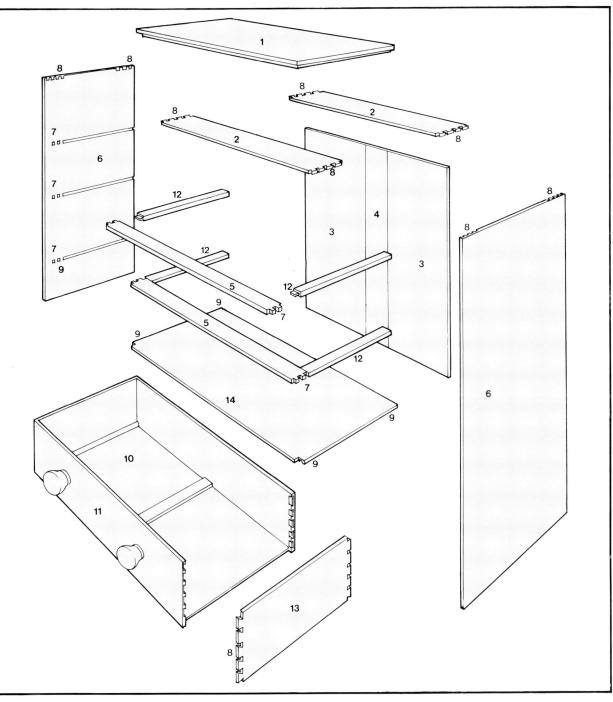

Above: The traditional carcass.
1. Top
2. Top carcass rail
3. Back panels
4. Vertical grooved strip
5. Rails, horizontal
6. Solid end
7. Mortise and tenon joints
8. Dovetail joints
9. Bottom shelf dovetail joints
10. Drawer bottom
11. Drawer front
12. Drawer runners
13. Drawer side
14. Bottom of carcass

bears a slot which is rectangular in section and fits into a recess carved into the other member. The two are then held together with glue or dowels.

Drawers are usually made using dovetail joints, strong joints specifically used where the rail has to take weight. In constructing the drawers themselves, the bottom should slide in from the back into grooves cut into the sides and front. The entire drawer should then sit and run on hardwood runners. The base of the drawer may be made of two panels joined together by means of a strip of wood, much as the back of the carcass is.

When faced with the problems of carcass repairs you should not take apart more than is

Right: The traditional mortise and tenon joint, where the tenon is inserted into the mortise, glued and then clamped

necessary. The repairs will usually fall into three main categories: the joints may have become loose or even broken, a whole section or panel may need to be replaced, or worn or shrunken parts may need to be replaced or repaired.

When dismantling, you may find it a good idea, particularly if you are inexperienced, to mark parts so that they are replaced in the correct positions. Do not strike the wood directly with a hammer or mallet. Instead, carefully knock the parts apart using a piece of scrap wood measuring at least two by one inches (50 by 25 mm), to ensure an even pressure and to prevent splitting. Apart from bruising the surface, the blow may crack a panel or break a joint.

Make sure before you do this that nothing else is holding the parts together. There might be a rail, back panel or moulding screwed or glued to both parts· which will prevent separation. There may even be nails from an earlier, unskilled restoration job. The separation of obstinate dovetail joints can sometimes be helped by damping and heating with a flat iron; simply apply the fairly hot iron on a damp cloth placed over the cleaned area (this also removes veneer). Do not flood with water, especially on the joints, as this may cause the wood to swell.

When the parts are separated, clean up the area, removing old, dried glue with a chisel. Broken dowels can be removed with a brace and bit or an electric drill. To remake a joint, use a gauge to ensure accurate measurements and a tenon saw for easy working. Loose joints should be reglued using suitable clamping pieces.

When dealing with broken parts, it is best to dismantle locally around the area. The most common breaks in main panels are known as split ends. These usually occur when a moulding has been used in the construction. Because the moulding is glued tightly to the ends of the panel it resists shrinking tendencies. The panel, on the other hand, splits when it dries out. Another fault is a failed joint. This occurs, again because of shrinkage, when two panels, usually in the sides, are held at the ends by mouldings. The gaps caused by open or failed joints are usually straight and parallel, but may be curved to the grain.

Above: The stub tenon, where the tenon is cut shorter so that it is not seen on the outside. It more effectively conceals the construction where strength is not so essential, as for example, on drawer guides. The mortise should only be about two-thirds the width of the wood

Left: A through dovetail joint, the strongest and most common joint used on corners, particularly those on drawers

usually includes worn edges (in friction with the runners), broken bottoms and loose joints. If the joints are loose it will be necessary to dismantle the drawer. Remove the bottom first, which may be held at the back by screws or nails and by small glue blocks along the underside edge of the drawer front. Chip the glue blocks away with a chisel. Tap out the sides from the front and back of the drawer using a piece of wood to prevent damage from the blows. Drawers are usually made with dovetail joints. Reglue the cleaned joints and reset, using a clamp if you feel it is necessary. Measure the diagonals for squareness. Replace the original glue blocks if these were present. When using the clamp do not place the metal directly on the wood. A piece of newspaper or plywood is the best separator to prevent scarring the wood.

If the edges of the drawer are worn it will be necessary to replace them. Cut a piece from the worn part making it as square as possible, and parallel to the top edge of the drawer. This can first be marked with a pencil and then cut with a chisel. Cut a replacement piece, a little larger than the damaged original, as you would when replacing a split end, and glue into position. When the glue has dried, plane the edge down level. A light coat of wax on all friction areas will help the drawer to run smoothly.

If the bottom of the drawer has split you may need to simply glue the split or repair it as a split end. In the first case you will have to do this while the drawer is dismantled. The underneath of the drawer bottom may have glue blocks which will need to be taken off and then replaced.

The most common faults found in doors are loose joints in the main framework, usually split mortises and split panels. You will have to dismantle to correct both of these faults, unless the panel split is a split-end type repair. If the joints are loose, dismantling will be easy. If not, make sure there are no nails holding anything and gently force the joints apart before cleaning off the old glue. Warps in the main framework can be cured by clamping it to another piece of wood and leaving it for a time. It is often just as easy to replace the piece, called a stile which is placed across the grain of the broken piece.

Clean out the split or joint using a saw or file. Prepare a strip of wood slightly thicker than the opening, and tapered in length if necessary. Plane it to a slight wedge shape so that it enters the opening easily in its length. Glue and tap it in with a small hammer and wait until dry.

When the glue has set, level the strip with a chisel, taking care to remove nothing from the adjoining surface. Sand to smooth.

Drawer runners often present a minor repair to the carcass. The chief fault is usually that of extensive wear where the lower edges of the drawers rub. The ends of the runners are normally scored into a trough by repeated use over the years. The runners may have to be repaired or replaced, depending on the extent of the damage. In either case, the runner will first of all have to be removed. They are usually held at the back with a screw and are stub-tenoned at the front, the outside edge being glued. A stub-tenon joint is essentially a smaller mortise and tenon joint. Simply undo the screw and prise the runner from the back. It is usually just as easy to replace the two outside runners as it is to carry out any repairs.

Some runners are not so complicated and are simply taken off and a replacement prepared and glued back on as Kenneth Davis shows in his repairs to the bottom part of the glass-fronted cupboard project on page 83.

The wear on the runners will usually be reflected in wear in the actual drawers. Damage to drawers

The tool kit

Repairs to broken legs may mean that new pieces will need to be spliced on or that the whole fractured leg will have to be replaced. Small pieces that have broken off can simply be reglued and filled ready for polishing, if necessary. The fracture may be repairable by regluing and strengthening with screws. The screws should be countersunk, that is the screw head should not be flush with the surface. You can do this with a brace and bit or by simply gouging a hole with a chisel. The former is more professional. The countersunk holes can then be filled (bevelled) by gluing in 'pellets' or tiny dowels.

Turned legs can present a special problem. Breaks in turned legs can sometimes be repaired by dowelling the two pieces together and then gluing. If the breakage is near the base of the leg you may be able to drill upwards through the leg from the foot up into the main part. The two parts should first be glued together. Insert a new dowel in the bored hole with glue. This repair requires some experience. If the leg needs to be replaced you can probably buy a replacement, either ordered or ready-made, at a good joiners or cabinetmakers. If you are lucky and skilled enough to be the owner of a lathe you can make the new leg yourself.

Chairs are the most used and abused piece of furniture in the home and so old chairs are likely to have many faults. Most of these are in the legs and the techniques already mentioned apply. Corner brackets can reinforce the leg if they are placed in the corners at the top end, near the seat.

The most common fault in chairs is loose joints. This usually happens between the back legs and seat rails, and results from the strain of people leaning back and tilting the chair on its back legs. You may have to dismantle the chairs if all the joints are loose. When you have done this clean away the old glue and reset the joints. You will need clamps to make sure the joints fit tightly while the glue is drying. A tourniquet made from a clothes line is an alternative to a clamp.

Another common fault is a broken rail in the underframe. The rail should be removed, without dismantling if possible. Again, this is almost always due to loose joints which need to be clean and reglued.

When part of a chair, or any other piece of furniture, needs to be replaced, you can use the old part as a template to mark and cut out the new part. Kenneth Davis demonstrates this technique when replacing a section of the top for a gate-leg table on page 67.

Right: An attractive cedar chest which is showing signs of wear and tear. One of the brass-bound corner pieces is missing—a specialist job to replace. It is also stained and scratched. The simple expedient of stripping and renewing the polish would turn it into a fine and valuable piece. A coat of wax will prevent more damage

Stripping and Finishing

The restoration of wood to its original lustre and brilliance is one of the joys of restoration. Here the various techniques are discussed and upholstery is introduced

Above: When buying pieces of furniture which have been stripped in bulk, usually in tanks of caustic soda, watch for signs of damage. This small drawer from a pine washstand has suffered extensive cracking. Made from a single piece of wood, the surface has reacted to drastic treatment. Although still usable for storage, the bottom is now weakened and will certainly need to be repaired at some time in the future

Besides a scraper, a paint brush or a grass brush will be of great value for stripping furniture of stains, polishes and paints. The paint brush should be regarded as expendable since once used it will be very difficult to clean to a standard suitable for painting. A grass brush made of coarse fibres is suitable for the application of bleaches and strippers which might destroy ordinary paint brushes.

Paint remover, methylated spirit or denatured alcohol, washing soda and vinegar are the main liquids needed for most stripping jobs. There are many abrasives available but you should be able to manage with coarse and fine steel wool, and some sheets of coarse and fine sandpaper. It is best to buy wet-and-dry sandpapers. By wetting the sheet before use you will avoid fractures which can scratch the surface of the furniture and may spoil the finish.

You can buy manufactured strippers from all do-it-yourself shops. These will have instructions regarding their use which should be followed implicitly. Washing soda should be used in solution of one part soda to ten parts water by weight.

There are two general procedures which you can use depending on whether the surface to be stripped is covered by a paint or a polish. To strip paint, apply the stripper and leave for a short period. When the surface begins to move, scrape in the direction of the grain. Several applications of stripper may be needed to reveal the bare wood. When all the paint has been removed, thoroughly rub down the piece of furniture with coarse steel wool and then scrub with soda diluted in hot water. Leave to dry and then wash again with diluted vinegar (approximately two teaspoons to 20 fluid ounces or half a litre of water). Leave to dry for 24 hours before sandpapering, working along the grain, as before. The surface should then be ready for staining and polishing.

To remove an old polish, cover the surface with methylated spirit or denatured alcohol and scrape when the surface begins to move. A second or third application may be necessary. Wipe dry with a cloth before rubbing with sandpaper along the grain. Remember to use a fine grade of sandpaper for this work.

Below: One sign that a piece has been stripped in a soda tank is 'bleeding'. The base of this piece is covered with a white crystalline deposit of soda which can be wiped away but will soon re-form. Cracking and shrinkage are also common faults, since the soda withdraws all natural oils from the wood

More difficult cases of old polish can be treated with caustic soda, but careful precautions are essential as it can burn badly. Rubber gloves should be worn, and the soda should be added to the water, not the other way round. It is advisable to do the job out of doors if possible. Caustic soda should not be used on veneers as it will soften the glue and pull the veneer away. After scraping, wash the wood with a little diluted vinegar to neutralize the caustic soda. The soda will, however, darken the wood considerably and this can be counteracted later by washing the piece of furniture with a peroxide bleach. Great care should be taken here as this process can irreparably damage the piece.

Finishing

Once you have cleaned the surface the next step is to stain it. Staining and finishing wood to give it colour and enhance the grain is perhaps the most enjoyable part of furniture restoration. After repairing a piece of furniture you will want to show it off to its best effect and to bring the dull but sound wood back to life.

It is sometimes necessary, particularly in the case of walnut or mahogany, to fill in the grain prior to staining and finishing. This is done by applying a wood filler paste, available in various brands. The filler can be thinned with white spirit or turpentine until it is the consistency and colour

of oatmeal. It should then be applied in a circular motion all over the surface of the piece with a piece of hessian, burlap or coarse rag. This should then be left for a few minutes and, when semi-dry, rubbed into the wood with a fresh piece of hessian or burlap. Do this by rubbing up and down the length of the grain. The grain pores of the wood should be uniformly filled and the surface free of all residues to avoid white-in-the-grain after staining (the white is left from the filler and, if present, the surface must be well sanded to remove it). Leave to dry for about 12 hours before lightly sanding with a fine paper. Most projects will not need filling, however, so you can normally proceed directly to staining or finishing as required.

There are three types of stains commonly in use and readily available: water stain, spirit stain and oil or wiping stain. Oil stain is the most popular of the three and is the easiest to use as it does not raise the grain when applied to the wood. Water raises the grain so that you should wet the surface, sand and then stain.

Before staining you can get the exact colour you want by testing the stain, which you may have either mixed yourself or bought, on scraps of matching wood. If the stain is too dark it can be diluted with white spirit or turpentine, while if it is too light more stain can be added.

Oil stains are powders which are mixed with turpentine, white spirits, naptha or similar oil products. They have great powers of penetration, but tend to build up over soft spots in the wood and for this reason they should be used sparingly. They should never be used on softwoods such as pine and spruce, or hardwoods such as beech or birch. The result could be patchy and uneven.

Oil stains are available ready-mixed under many brand names some of which are intermixable if you wish to achieve a special colour. However, by using white spirit or turpentine you can easily make them up yourself. They are fairly quick-drying and depth can be built up by repeated applications. To gain maximum adhesion leave the piece for about 18–24 hours between each coat.

Spirit stains are best for colouring in small patches but tend to be uneven over large areas. They consist of dyes and translucent pigments dissolved in denatured alcohol or methylated spirits. They can be added to French polish to impart more colour.

Water stains can be 'earth' colours, which are effective and cheap and reflect the browns of natural earth colours, but the most common are aniline dyes which give a brilliant effect and do not fade because of their deep penetration. The earth colours tend to fill the surface pores only, but they are suitable for certain types of old furniture. Water stains raise the grain a great deal but this can be corrected with sanding and the use of Vandyke brown dye crystals. The crystals should be diluted in water with a little ammonia, turpentine or white spirit to give a darkish oak stain.

After filling and staining you can coat the wood by French polishing. It is necessary to begin by sanding with a fine paper before applying the polish with a brush or the pad described below.

The most popular polish, French polish, can be bought under a great number of brand names. There are many other types available such as pale, white and translucent polish. French polish is hard and dries quickly. If you wish to darken it you can add Bismarck brown, a powder which, despite its name, is red when dissolved in polish. Experiment with the quantities until you achieve the required colour.

After sanding, dip the pad into the polish, being careful not to make it too wet. The pad should be

Above: The decorative parts are often missing from old furniture. Brass reproduction handles such as these can replace them. The selection shows a reproduction of an early plate handle (top), an eighteenth-century Sheraton handle (left of centre row), a swan neck and a Georgian lion head. The bottom handle is a Queen Anne type

Above left: The range of effects from staining and bleaching mahogany. On the left, stains achieved with oil, the central strip has been bleached, and on the right, water stained

Stripping and finishing

Below: Fine carving is worth restoring and preserving. A small piece of matching wood should be glued on to this ornamental carving on a cabinet to replace a chip, and then carved to match. Staining and polishing will restore it completely

made from a wad of cotton wool rolled and then covered with a fine, porous rag, such as a clean handkerchief or piece of old sheet.

Rub the polish on to the wood, working first with the grain and then in circular movements. If the pad becomes sticky add a small drop of linseed oil to soften it. The more you rub the polish into the wood, the more lustrous the finish. When you feel that you have polished sufficiently finish off with the pad, using the polish without the oil.

Leave the piece to dry for about one hour before sanding with a fine paper lightly covered with linseed oil. Then wipe the wood dry with a rag and repeat the process. Finally, finish off with straight up and down movements along the grain.

Wax polishing is the best way to complete the finish. Traditionally, wax polishes were made from a mixture of turpentine, beeswax and carnauba wax. Modern waxes contain silicone compounds and are possibly superior as they protect against scratching or marking. This type of polishing is not particularly durable on raw wood so it is advisable first to apply a thin layer of polish or boiled linseed oil diluted with an equal amount of turpentine or white spirit and used sparingly. Softwoods are generally not suitable for oiling.

In many cases you do not need to do a complete finish and the piece of furniture may only need to be 'revived'. A simple method is to lightly sand the piece with a fine paper, then wash with a weak vinegar or detergent solution and then French or wax polish.

Decorative Parts

Besides repairs to the main parts of the furniture, you will also come across damage to the decorative features, which are often so vital to the quality and character of the piece. Decorative parts might include bracket feet, cocked beads, mouldings, banding and veneers as well as inlays, scrolls or carving.

Bracket feet can be repaired fairly easily. If the break is a new one the broken edges will be sharp, if old they will be dirty and chipped. A new break can simply be glued and refitted. The break line might be very obvious if you glue an old break, however, and you will probably have to make a replacement. This can be done by making a template, drawn on a piece of thin white cardboard, from the other foot. Cut this shape out with a fret or coping saw, sandpaper the new foot and refit, ready for staining. All the legs can then be reinforced by blocks of wood screwed behind the bracket.

Cocked beads are found round the main panels of drawers and on the outside edges of the main framework of doors in some pieces of furniture. These are easy to repair. Merely reglue if you still have the broken piece or insert a new piece using the same type of wood. Glue and sand down flush with the old beading.

A fairly common problem is a broken or missing moulding. It is called 'stuck' moulding if it is worked into the piece of wood at the edges. This is most commonly found on table tops. Applied mouldings are glued on to the surface.

Stuck moulding usually suffers from small indents or it may be broken at the corner, particularly on a table. The damaged corner should be cut off and a replacement made. The replacement should be cut wider and thicker than the original so that you can plane it to shape. The edge to be connected to the corner should be planed flat so that it can form a good glued joint. When the glue is set, plane down with a modern light plane so that it matches the rest of the moulding.

Applied moulding will often have missing sections. Cut the broken edges square to receive new pieces. You can buy lengths of moulding from a good timber merchant, and these can be cut as required and then fitted into place and sanded flush.

Damage to veneer can range from the smallest blemish to the major problem of repairing marquetry. When dealing with veneer faults remember that you can buy sheets of veneer from specialists. Broken veneer on corners and edges is a common fault. Deal with this by cutting the damaged veneer —always across the end grain—with a knife, at an angle of about 45°, so that the piece to be inserted will be diamond-shaped. Clean

Below: The central feature of this modern dining room is a huge Edwardian table which has been stripped to reveal the beautiful grain of the old pine, with chairs to match. A Victorian mahogany sideboard adds to the room's warmth

old glue away. Insert the new piece of veneer (cut a little longer than the original) using glue and a G or C clamp. Level the overhanging veneer when the glue has dried. The grain of the old veneer piece should be matched as closely as possible when buying your new veneer.

Veneer can 'bubble' when the old glue decays. This can be dealt with by cutting the veneer with a thin, sharp knife so that the cut is as fine as possible. Use a ruler to make it straight. Using the knife, spread the glue under the two edges of the cut. A palette knife would be the ideal tool. Clamp the glued piece, protecting it with a sheet of newspaper or cloth.

Large areas of veneer can be removed by covering it with wet rags and then placing a very hot, flat iron on top. Remove as much of the old glue as you can with a hot damp cloth, scraping if necessary. Replace or reglue the old piece when it has dried remembering to clamp it.

The repairing of inlays, scrolls and carvings can be carried out by the amateur if they are confined to regluing. If a new piece is required, you will probably need to have it replaced by a professional.

Carving is a specialist job. However, it is interesting to try and some people have a natural aptitude for it although they may lack the technical experience. If you wish to try it, you will need a set of carving tools. Try the simpler projects such as leaves, flower petals and motifs. Carvings should be glued back on to the piece of furniture.

In most restoration jobs there will be a part to be replaced which you may have to cut yourself. This covers a wide variety of jobs ranging from remaking a mortise and tenon joint to cutting bracket feet. The general procedure is to lay the part on a piece of cardboard and mark its shape in pencil. The copy should be slightly bigger than the original so that you can plane and sand it into a good fitting position. Cut out the pattern with a sharp knife. Place the cardboard on a new piece of wood and follow the outline. Cut with a pad or jig saw or with a fret or coping saw. Sand the cut piece and match constantly until you have a good fit.

Joints can be made by cutting with a tenon saw. You could use a template for a large dovetail joint. For a broken mortise and tenon you will need to clean out the mortise. Measure the tenon with a gauge and cut a piece twice its length. This can then be recessed by gluing into a new mortise on the rail or piece on which the tenon was originally built. Clamp while waiting for the glue to dry.

Broken rails are fairly easy to replace, even when you have to make a tenon on both ends. When remaking a rail you may not need to make a template since you can simply mark out the shape onto another piece of wood. Cut with a jig saw or pad saw. An interesting variation to replacement is shown in the project on the chest of drawers. Parts of the bottom, suffering from dry rot, can be cut away to form new legs which, with some blocks to reinforce, are sturdy and attractive.

Right: There are a number of tools common to both upholstery and woodwork. The tools illustrated here are specially adapted to the various techniques and are indispensable.
1. *Upholsterer's needle (250–300 mm)*
2. *Cabriole hammer*
3. *Curved upholsterer's needle*
4. *Tack lifter*
5. *Ripping chisel*
6. *Pincers*
7. *Web strainer*
8. *Mallet*
9. *Upholstery shears*

Upholstery

Upholstery is a combination of soft furnishing and carpentry. It is a wide subject and there are a variety of techniques to deal with a range of furniture, from small dining room chairs to larger settees. Perhaps the best introduction for the beginner is to refurbish the drop-in seat of a dining-room chair.

Called 'stuffed' furniture when it first appeared in France, upholstered chairs and sofas did not become widely used until the spiral spring was made in quantity in the middle of the Victorian period. The techniques developed in Britain at that time are still in use today. New techniques and materials, such as rubber or plastic webbing and foam sheets in place of springs, fail to give the same finished appearance to old furniture.

Many of the tools used for upholstery are modified carpenters' tools. In this sense they are specialized and, although you can improvise, it is worth buying the proper tools, of good quality, if you intend undertaking a major renovation.

The most specialized tool is the web strainer or stretcher. This is extremely useful for stretching webbing as tightly as possible across the frame of a chair or chaise longue. Webbing can be pulled tight with the hands but since it is one of the most important parts of upholstering it is just as well to use the strainer to ensure maximum tension.

Tacks will be needed to attach most of the

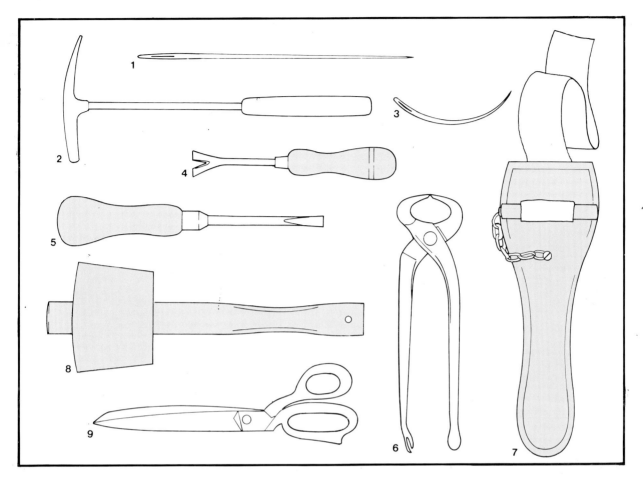

coverings to the repaired frame. Buy the sort with wide heads for attaching the webbing. For the main upholstery you will need three-eighths inch (9 mm) fine long tacks. These can be half inch (12 mm) if the cover fabric is thick. The webbing should be attached with half-inch tacks for chairs, and five-eighths inch (15 mm) tacks for sofas.

A cabriole hammer, with a swan-like neck can be used where a lot of show-wood is displayed. Show-wood is the part of the frame which is polished, or sometimes carved, and which acts as a 'frame' for the cover fabric. The small head of the cabriole hammer will reduce the chances of damaging the show-wood but if you feel confident use an ordinary tack or fret hammer. A tack lifter, which has a forked, claw head, is ideal for removing tacks which have rusted into the wood. A mallet and ripping chisel can be used for taking out particularly stubborn tacks. Blunt by design, the tip of the chisel will not damage the frame.

A sharp pair of upholstery shears, for cutting webbing and fabric, will save you time and give a better finish to your work. Upholsterers' needles, heavier and stronger than sewing needles, are pointed at both ends so that they can go through thick stuffing with ease. These are used mainly with flax twine. Use a ten or twelve inch (250 or 300 mm) needle for the heavier work and a curved three inch (75 mm) needle for finer jobs, such as edges and pleating. The curved needle is also used for stitching the springs to the webbing.

Coiled springs are used in most forms of sprung seating. These are available in different sizes and gauges, ranging from quite large springs for the seats of easy chairs to smaller ones used for the backs and arms of bigger reclining chairs, and for the seats of dining room chairs. Zig-zag and tension springs are sometimes used in smaller chairs.

You will also need various material which will include the covering fabric, jute webbing, black hessian or burlap, canvas, coconut and horsehair fibres and three-ply sisal cord for tying springs in larger chairs. If you are buttoning a sofa you will need upholstery buttons. These have to be covered with matching pieces from the cover fabric.

When you are stripping old upholstery it is best to proceed slowly, layer by layer. Impatient tearing may damage materials which you can use again. Note how each layer is attached to the other.

If the upholstery is in good condition it may only be necessary to repair it in parts or merely to remove the cover. Old covers should always be taken off and should never be merely re-covered, as the dust and grime of the old will eventually seep through to the new. When only the webbing of a sprung chair has broken it is sometimes possible to make a repair from beneath, without removing the covering and other layers. This will involve taking off the underside hessian or burlap and removing all the old webbing, knocking out the tacks and cutting the twine lacing.

Project 1: A Pine Desk

The complete renovation of this old pine desk involves waxing, repairing split ends, restoring the finish to fittings, stripping painted wood, removing scratches and household stains, and colouring the pine.

This pine desk presents some of the commonest faults to be remedied in antique furniture. The desk is stained with a dark colour which gives it a heavy appearance. It would look its best if stripped to the pine and coated with a wax polish to protect the wood and recapture the beauty of the grain of the aged pine. This dark stain has also been coated on the door handle and other fittings. They will need to be cleaned and buffed back to their original state or replaced as in this project. The door handle is damaged and needs replacing.

Another fault is the chipped wood on the front of the drawer. Often small faults on drawers involve the replacement of veneer. They are easy to correct. When the veneered surface has developed a blister, it is almost certain that the glue used to fix the veneer has finally decayed. To repair this, cut through the blister with a very thin-bladed, sharp knife. A scalpel, which you can buy in an art shop or a department store, would be the ideal tool. Using the blade of the knife, spread some glue under the sides of the blister, covering as much area under the loose veneer as you can.

To press down the glued blister, warm a small hammer in hot water and press it on the outside edges of the blister, gradually working into the centre. Wipe off the excess glue and put a length of adhesive tape along the line of the original cut. This will prevent the edges from curling upwards while the glue is drying. After 24 hours remove the tape by dampening it, and clean the repair with fine sandpaper. Be very careful when doing this not to damage the veneer.

If a piece of veneer has to be replaced, follow the method which is demonstrated in the diagram on page 84.

Splits in the end panels of desks and other heavy pieces of old furniture are also common. In this case, there is no need to dismantle the carcass to remove the end itself. The method of dealing with this is shown in the diagram on page 38.

Splits in the actual panel are invariably tapered and follow the grain. This repair will be easier if you enlarge the width of the narrow end of the gap. The new insert is then shaped accordingly and glued into place. Then trim down the strip of wood. Splits along the joint of two panels are generally parallel and the insert requires little or no shaping. You will get a more professional finish if you match the grain of the insert to the original wood.

When the desk has been stripped, wax should be used as a finish. There are two kinds of wax used on old furniture, wax used exclusively as a finish and wax which is a 'dressing' on top of a stain. Beeswax is the best type to use for finishing.

Beeswax may be bought in block or flake form. It should be covered in turpentine and heated until the wax dissolves. Great care should be taken when doing this. A much easier method is simply to buy a proprietary brand of wax polish. For pine the wax should be uncoloured. The most important factor when waxing is not to apply second or third coats before the previous coat has completely dried. A waxed surface can be greatly improved by briskly rubbing it with a rag and then wiping with a duster.

After stripping the polish from a piece of furniture, you may find that there are a number of scratches, bruises, glass marks or ink stains underneath the paint. This may have been the reason for painting it. Scratches can usually be dealt with by sanding with a fine sandpaper dipped in linseed oil. For deeper scratches, simply fill with wax and then rub level with fine sandpaper. To remove bruises, lie a damp cloth over the bruise and place a hot domestic iron on top of it. Glass marks, like heat and water marks, can usually be eliminated by rubbing with linseed oil and turpentine mixed in equal quantities. The oil can be removed with vinegar.

Ink stains can often be removed by using an ordinary domestic chlorine bleach. Apply this only over the area requiring treatment. If bleach should fail you can use a proprietary brand of diluted nitric or oxalic acid. This will turn the stain white and this in turn can be removed with a proprietary brand of camphorated oil. You should not use any of these materials in the presence of children as they are poisonous and may be imbibed accidentally on the finger.

The major part of renovating this pine desk consists in stripping the old dark paint. Brush on a

To fill the split in the end of the desk, clean it out with a file or chisel and then prepare a piece of wood matching the length and widest part of the hole, but about quarter of an inch (six millimetres) deeper than the split. If the gap tapers slightly, it will be necessary to shape the insert correspondingly, using a surform smoothing plane. Chisel the wedge until it fits tightly enough so that you can hammer it gently into place, after glueing all edges, using a small cross-pein or pin hammer.

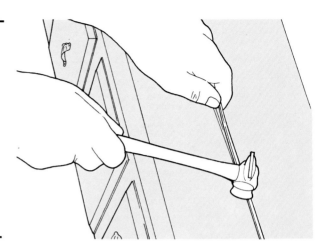

When the glue has dried, trim down the new insert, being careful not to damage the original surface of the desk. Use a bevelled wood chisel, paring thin slices at a time. Never try to take too much off at once as the chisel will rip along the grain of the inserted wood and you may have to start all over again. When you have pared flush, sand to get a really good finish. Check that the surfaces are level with the straight edge of a ruler or with the blade of a try-square.

It is sometimes necessary when restoring old furniture to remove the screws. You may need to clean paint from them, or they might prevent access to parts of the furniture you wish to repair. Using a screwdriver, take off all the handles and fittings. With some furniture, you may find that the screws are rusted and you cannot gain purchase when unscrewing. Carefully prise them out with pliers or pincers.

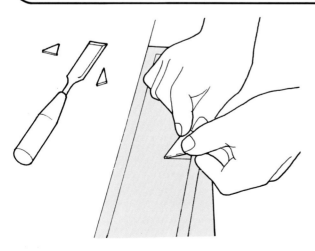

To repair chips to the wood on the drawer front, cut a new piece of matching wood, or, if the chip is shallow, use a piece of pine veneer. Glue the area to be repaired and insert the piece carefully. Wipe the area free of excess glue and allow to dry overnight. Sand the insert flush with the drawer front.

paint remover and then leave it for a short period until the surface begins to move or cockle. Then, using a scraper, remove the residues. You will need several applications of paint remover.

The important technique is to let the stripper do most of the work. You should not have to exert a great deal of force. If the surface of the paint does not cockle easily, recoat liberally with the remover. If you have to exert too much pressure when scraping, you are likely to damage the surface.

It is always a good idea when stripping to place the piece of furniture on some sheets of newspaper. A cloth would also be useful for wiping the residues of paint off the scraper when it

Above: Kenneth Davis is using a steel scraper to remove the residues of paint after it has started to cockle and rise. Notice that he is working along the grain and is being careful not to allow the scraper to dig into the wood

When all the paint is stripped from the desk, prepare the surface for staining by using a sheet of coarse sandpaper wrapped round a simple wooden block and sand the desk along the direction of the grain. Sand until the surface is perfectly clean and then wipe down the dust with a damp cloth. Leave to dry and then repeat the process with a fine sandpaper. Wipe down again. When dry the surface is ready for staining.

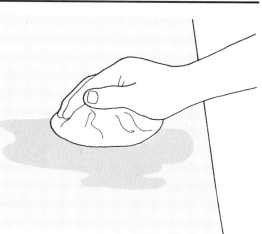

Staining is one of the most satisfying parts of restoration. You will need a home-made pad, described on page 32. For a pine desk use an uncoloured wax polish to heighten the natural colour of the wood. Using the pad, spread the wax in smooth, circular strokes. Leave for 24 hours after you have covered the whole desk. Then smooth the surface with fine steel wool before applying the final coat of wax.

Use fine wire wool and paint remover to clean all of the handles and fittings. To remove fine flecks of paint from inaccessible places you can finish the cleaning with methylated spirit or denatured alcohol. When clean, buff the fittings and handles to a shine.

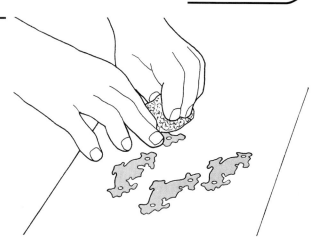

To replace the slightly damaged handle, buy a suitable replacement and mark its position before drilling the screw holes. It is probably best to remove the drawers and door so that you drill with the weight exerted downwards, ensuring a straighter hole and avoiding damage. Handles can then be screwed on.

begins to pile up. Do not dispose of the paper and cloth by burning. They will be highly inflammable.

When the paint is removed, the surface is thoroughly washed with soda dissolved in hot water, and coarse steel wool, although a scrubbing brush would do as well. After the surface has dried, it is again washed with methylated spirit or denatured alcohol and allowed to dry before being washed down with diluted vinegar. It should be left to dry for 24 hours before the surface is sanded to prepare for waxing.

Some proprietary brands of paint removers and strippers may carry specific instructions as to the best material you should use to clean them from the wood. In most cases this is methylated spirit or denatured alcohol but always check. It may not be suitable for mixing with the chemical in the remover.

The stripped surface when cleaned down may look attractive and give the piece of furniture a new lease of life. However, you may not be so lucky in every project you undertake. You may wish to lighten the colour of the wood still further or to darken it to hide various scratches and stains which you cannot remove to your satisfaction.

To lighten the pine use a peroxide No. 2 bleach with an equal volume of water. Bleaching will be necessary if you have to take the drastic and unpleasant step of removing the old paint or stain with a solution of caustic soda. This should only be used when all else has failed as it can cause

Above: The waxed, natural pine now has a beauty which would look attractive in any home. The shiny fittings serve to enhance the colour of the wood and are not merely utilitarian. Many similar desks have been covered in layers of paint and may be unrecognizable as fine old pieces of pine furniture. Therefore amateur restorers should be on the lookout for such hidden treasure

nasty burns and should be handled with care. If you are unused to these substances, take advice before you use them and make sure that you know how to treat burns should you have an accident.

To increase the colour, buy a dye or tint and mix it with the heated wax. There are many proprietary brands of coloured wax on the market and you may be lucky in finding the one you want without having to mix them. Remember when applying the mixture that each coat will darken the colour even more. This should be taken into consideration when selecting and mixing. Test each combination on an old piece of similar wood and allow it to dry before making your final decision.

Another method of deepening colour is to apply a single coat of stain before waxing. The best material to use in this case is French polish. If you do not bring it to too fine a shine, it will be an excellent base for waxing. It has the added advantage of toning and polishing new pieces of wood so that they are effectively disguised.

Project 2: Three Chairs

This project presents three old chairs to be restored according to their different faults. Woodworm is treated in an old oak chair, legs are strengthened, the seat of a cane chair is renewed, and an old dining room chair is re-upholstered

Left: The three chairs before restoration. The oak chair has a broken rail and loose joints but is in overall good condition. The upholstered chair needs a lot of work as it has splayed front legs, broken tenons and ruined upholstery. The cane chair needs recaning as well as a new rail

Chairs take more strain and abuse than any other piece of furniture. The types of repair will depend on the individual chair as they are all constructed in so many different ways. The most common trouble is that the joints have broken or become loose. The rails, including those of the seat, can also become loose because they have had to take too much weight.

The first thing you should do with a chair you are about to tackle is to inspect it. Don't take the whole thing apart just because of one or two broken rails. Only take apart what is absolutely necessary. If it is possible to open the joint of the broken rail or leg, then deal with the repair locally.

A more serious form of damage is a rail which has been split in the middle. In this case it is often necessary to replace the old rail with a new one which you can easily make yourself.

The main problem with local repairs to rails and joints is how to get the joints back into place. The rail can be sprung back if the original joint is a tenon joint which is still intact. Another way of dealing with this is by making a loose tenon. The loose tenon is made and fitted into the leg so that it protrudes about two inches (five centimetres) after you have glued it into the original mortise in the legs (remembering to clean out the mortise first). Another mortise is cut in the rail but is cut open on the underside. Glue both the tenon and rail mortise. Slide the rail down onto the tenon. It should then be clamped.

Broken legs may be easy to make from a template but with the more complicated turned leg you may have to buy or have a replacement made, unless you have a lathe. If a square-sectioned leg is broken it is often possible to repair rather than replace it. It is usually better to splice on a new piece rather than just glue the two pieces together. Wood of the same kind must be used and the join should be diagonal or tapered so as to give more gluing surface and consequently a stronger joint. You can gain even more strength if you screw the two pieces after they have been glued. Drill holes large enough to receive the whole screw head so that it can be hidden by a wooden plug glued into position. Smooth the plugs with sandpaper after the glue has set.

Apart from a broken rail, the faults and damage to this oak chair are minor. The legs of the chair are slightly loose, but can be repaired by inserting dowels in the joints. The split in the seat can be prevented from opening any further by placing a strip of canvas underneath it. The woodworm holes in the back rail need treatment by filling either with sawdust or commercial wood-filler.

Replacing the new rail is not so difficult because the legs are already loose at the joints. This means that a rail can be inserted by pulling the legs slightly apart. In many cases chairs either have to be taken apart completely or have a loose tenon constructed. Another way to deal with this problem is to cut a stub tenon, at an angle of about 30 degrees, in the upper corner of the top of the tenon. This enables the tenon to be fitted into the mortise without bruising the legs.

When the chair is repaired, the new rail should be match stained and the woodworm holes filled before wax polishing.

Left: The oak chair is infested with woodworm and the holes can be seen on the back rail. Treatment is simple with products easily available to the amateur. The side rail is completely missing and will have to be replaced with a piece of matching wood. You may be able to find an old rail on a useless chair to match the one you are restoring

The new rail roughly measures from the outside edge of one leg to the outside edge of the opposite leg. Cut along the grain with a tenon saw. When you are making this measurement ensure that splayed or broken legs do not distort the accuracy of the pencil mark. Although it is only a rough calculation, this kind of inaccuracy can make the cutting of the tenons more difficult.

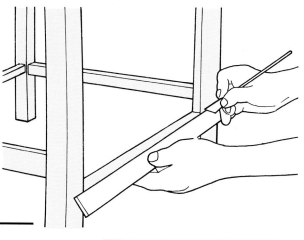

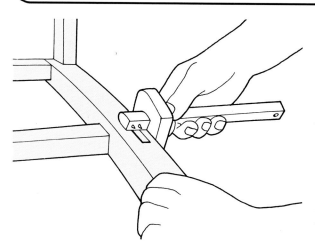

Before marking the cutting outlines of the tenons on the new piece of wood, measure the old mortise in the chair leg with a mortise gauge. Set the two pins on the gauge to the width of the mortise. Then mark the outline for the tenon on the new rail, using the pins to scratch the wood. You can make the marking clearer if you pencil over the scratches. This will enable you to see the marking even if it becomes covered with sawdust.

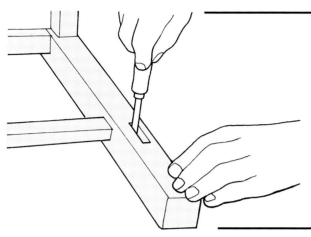

The old mortise holes in the legs can be cleaned out with a bradawl or small screwdriver. The important thing is to remove all the old glue from the corners and bottom edges of the joint. If the broken tenon of the old rail is still firmly glued into the mortise you will need a chisel to remove it. Shave off small pieces at a time with the thin chisel, making sure that you do not enlarge or cut into the rim edges of the mortise.

Now set about sawing the tenons using a tenon saw. Place the rail in a bench vice in a slightly slanted position as the picture shows. This can make the sawing position more comfortable. The tenon should be cut on the outside of the pencil marks to ensure that it fits tightly into the mortise. If it is too large you can always chisel it to size. You cannot add to it if it is too small.

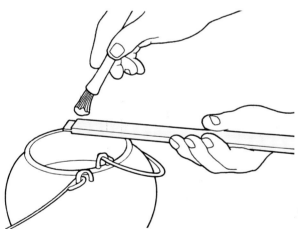

When the tenon is cut and sanded to size, cover it with glue smeared on with a paint brush. Apply a little glue to the mortise.

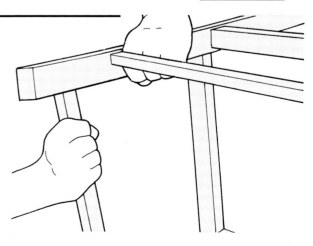

The glued rail is then inserted into the mortises by very gently prising the legs apart. Never pull the legs of any piece of furniture you are repairing too roughly.

When the rail has been inserted and all excess glue wiped away with a piece of cloth, clamp the chair with a sash clamp. Place two pieces of wood under the feet of the clamp to protect the chair when it is wound tightly into place. The ends of the clamp should be placed directly opposite the repaired joints. If you do not want to buy or hire a sash clamp you can make a tourniquet of rope or cord. Bind the rope twice round the chair legs and tie a knot. Near a corner, insert a piece of dowel between the strands and twist it tight.

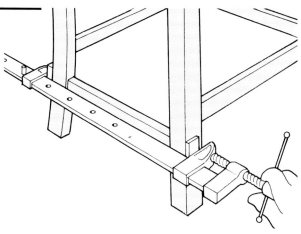

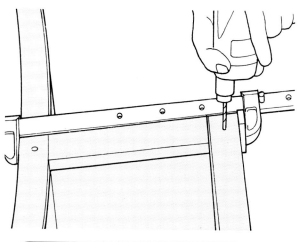

Bore holes into the sides of the legs so that dowel strengtheners can be used to reinforce the loose joints. Cut a piece of dowel about a quarter of an inch (six millimetres) shorter than the hole. Make a second cut along the length of the dowel and widen it with a file to form a V shape. This will allow excess glue to escape. The hole should be plugged with matching wood and glued into place after the dowel glue has dried. Sand.

The slight split in the chair can be repaired with a strip of canvas which acts as a reinforcement, preventing the split from opening further. For this type of hidden repair, plywood or even hardboard could be substituted for the traditional canvas. Linen is also used as a substitute. Cut the canvas into shape and glue. Apply glue to the underside of the seat. Then press the canvas firmly into place, squeezing out excess glue.

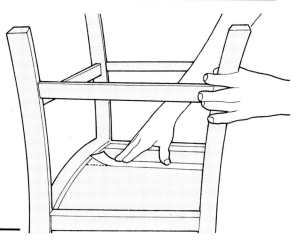

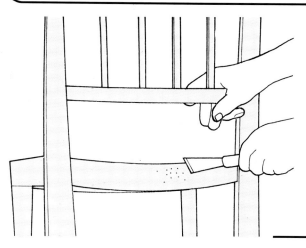

There are several ways to treat woodworm and, more particularly, woodworm holes. The first step is to spray the holes with an aerosol insecticide. This has to be done in the spring, in time for the mating of the insects. To fill the holes, mix some sawdust and glue and work it into the holes. Woodfiller, stained with a matching colour, is a good alternative. The finished chair on the right is now restored for many more years of use.

Project 2

Right: The cane chair before restoration. One of the rails needs replacing, staining and polishing, but the major part of the restoration involves complete recaning using a technique which seems difficult but is simplicity itself

The restoration of a cane chair involves two processes: the woodwork to replace the missing rail and the canework.

The first step is to repair the missing rail and prepare the chair for caning. To prepare the chair all the old cane has to be removed and, if necessary, the chair must be repolished and restained. This should never be done after the caning is completed as it will cause discolouration to the canework. Also, the holes for the insertion of the cane lengths must be cleaned out so that the new pattern will not be distorted in appearance.

Caning requires few tools and many of these are already household items. Scissors are useful for cutting the cane. Any size is suitable as long as they are reasonably sharp. A small hammer would be ideal for tapping the pegs into the holes although you can probably get by without this. Tapping the pegs with a hammer instead of pushing hard with the hand will ensure that the pegs do not fall out and spoil the part of the weave you are working on. A small bodkin or even an upholstery needle will help if your fingers are not particularly nimble at weaving cane in small spaces. You will definitely need something to clear the holes when carrying out the preparatory work. This can be an improvised tool, such as a nail, a small screwdriver, a metal knitting needle or even a piece of metal coathanger with the point sawn off. The most important tool is a cutting knife. It will enable you to cut with great precision and in areas where other cutters cannot reach.

You will also need pegs for jamming the cane lengths into the holes temporarily while you are weaving. Any pointed sticks or dowels about two inches (five centimetres) long are suitable. Basketwood cane is ideal.

The cane used for chair seats and backs comes from a rattan creeper which grows to enormous lengths in south-east Asia. It is sold in handyman and artists' supply shops in two types and six sizes. Blue tie, the kind of cane normally used for antique furniture, is the best quality but it is expensive. Red tie is cheaper and is suitable for most projects.

Cane sizes range from the thinner number one to the thick number six. Numbers two and four are the sizes used for most chairs. The distance between the holes, measured from centre to centre, determines the size to use. The usual distance is half an inch (one centimetre), making it suitable for numbers two and four cane. If the holes are less than half an inch apart it is advisable to use numbers two and three because they are easier to weave in confined spaces. For very fine work, numbers one and two should be used.

There is another consideration to take into account when making your choice of cane sizes—cost and economy. One bundle of cane is more than enough material to cane a chair seat. If you buy two sizes of cane for one chair you will have at least half of each left over. For this reason you should choose to weave with only one size. However, what you gain in economy you will lose in quality and finish. A one-size cane weave does not look as attractive as a two- or three-size weave. And the material left over could be used for another project.

One of the simplest weaves for chairs is called the Seven Step Tradition. The seven steps in the weave are as follows:
1. First verticals
2. First horizontals
3. Second verticals
4. Woven horizontals
5. First diagonals
6. Second diagonals
7. Beading

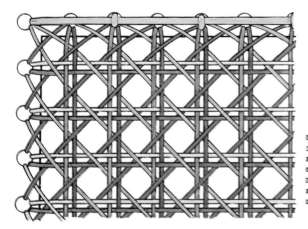

Left: The Seven Step Tradition is here shown in diagrammatic form, the colours indicate the various steps

1. First verticals
2. First horizontals
3. Second verticals
4. Woven horizontals
5. First diagonals
6. Second diagonals
7. Beading

Prepare the chair by cutting away all of the old, ragged cane. Pull out any small nails or wooden pegs which may have been used to pin or jam the cane. You may find that it is easier to clear away the rest of the cane left in the holes by cutting at the tied strands under the rails of the seat and pulling them free. Do not mark the chair with the knife.

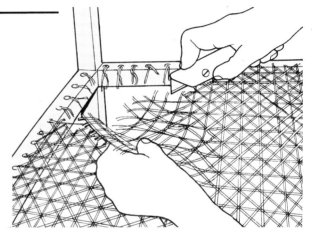

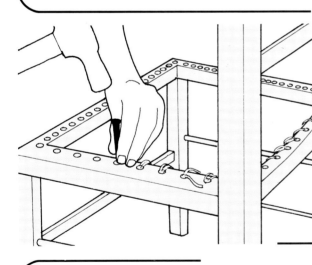

Clean out each hole individually with a blunt piece of wire, a long nail or a punch. It is important that the holes are cleared completely to prevent the new cane from sticking. When they are cleaned, locate the centre front and centre back holes. Lightly mark them with a pencil.

To replace the broken rail, measure a length of dowel to the required diameter with at least one and a half inches (four centimetres) extra for the tenons. After it is cut, sanded and fitted, glue the new rail into the mortises by slightly spreading the legs apart. Apply a sash clamp and wipe away excess glue. Now sand the new rail and stain it to match the rest of the chair. The whole chair should then be lightly 'cut' with fine steel wool, wax polished and french polished to revive the finish and bring out the inlays.

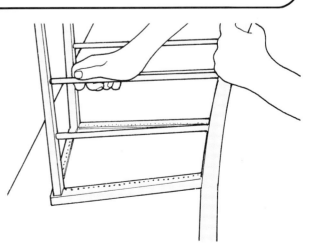

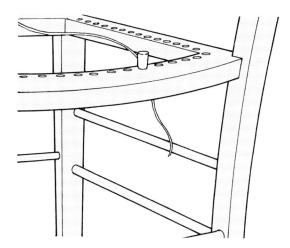

*Above: The chair after the first verticals have
been inserted. The two strands at each side
are strung between holes at the front and the
sides. This means that the strands are kept
parallel*

The lighter cane is usually used for steps one to
four, changing to the heavier size for steps five
and six. Beading is normally done with sizes two
and six cane. If you have any doubts about which
sizes to use, take the old cane which has been cut
from the chair to the shop for reference. It is a
good idea to make a drawing of the old weave
before you cut it away. Make this a detailed
drawing marking the direction of each strand, the
number of holes and the number of canes in each
hole. Do each step in different colours. If the
chair is old it is probable that there will be no
beading surrounding the weave. Beading is a
relatively modern addition to the art of weaving.

Some professionals like to wet the cane before
starting work. If you are a beginner, it might be a
good idea to do so. Cane is very brittle and unless
you are used to handling it, it is liable to split and
crack.

It is inadvisable to soak the cane as this may
cause discolouration. It is better, and just as
effective, to wet the cane as you work. You can
do this by passing it through a bowl of water just
before you weave it. If the cane dries out too
quickly while you are weaving you should wet

your fingers and pass them on the underside of
the material, not the shiny side.

You should be careful not to step or kneel on
the cane as you work as this will cause it to split
lengthways. Even a tiny split is liable to creep up
the whole length of the strand. Throw away all
split pieces, they will make the work look
unsightly. Keep checking the work as you go so
as to avoid having to unravel the weave.

The cane should also be dampened for tying in
the ends. Tying in is done when you have finished
one length of strand and are starting a new length.
The new end is passed twice around a short
strand spanning the small space between two
holes on the underside of the seat frame. It is then
tightened by pulling gently. If you tie in the ends
as you work you will not need many pegs for
jamming the cane in the holes and you will not
have as much finishing to do at the end of the
weaving.

The alternative is not to worry about tying in
the ends until you have finished and there are
quite a lot of pegs holding various lengths of
cane. The cane should be tied before you remove
the pegs. To make this easier you can dampen the
cane. Using scissors, cut each length of cane to a
point. Thread the end twice around a loop spanning two holes, in the same way as described for
tying in during weaving. Then take the end back
under itself, pull tight and cut off the excess. If
there are three or four ends coming out of the
same hole you can use not only the loops immediately on each side but the next ones along
as well.

In the past, nails, basket cane or wooden pegs
were used to jam the strands permanently in the
holes. These were never removed. But they tend
to give an unsightly finish. The addition of the
beading step has made them unnecessary. Beading gives not only a very professional and polished
finish but also strength and durability so that the
cane does not slip and sag when subjected to
weight over a period of time. For this reason it is
preferable to use a grade six cane for the beading.
If the holes are larger than an eighth of an inch
(three millimetres) then grade six will be necessary to cover them.

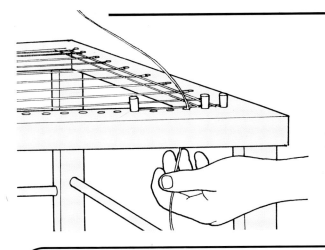

Next, string the horizontals from side to side, starting at the front and working straight through to the back without interruption. (Step 2) The horizontal canes should lie on top of the vertical strands. This will provide the basic frame for the diagonals.

Insert pegs as you string the horizontals. This will ensure that the strands are taut, but not overstretched. Jam the pegs into the last four or five holes you have used moving them as you work the strands from side to side, so that they 'travel' with the caning. Do not remove pegs which are holding loose ends.

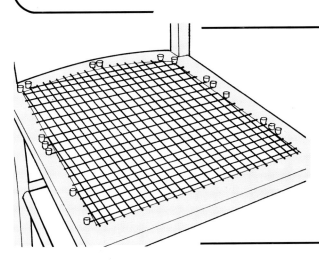

When all the horizontals are in place, the tension of the strands should be fairly tight and even but not at stretching point. The shiny side of both horizontals and verticals should be uppermost.

To place the second verticals, (Step 3) follow almost the same procedure as for the first, beginning at the middle and working out to either side. The second verticals are laid on top of the previous two steps but they should not lie directly on top of the first verticals, but parallel to them with a slight space between. Lay the strands to the right of the first verticals.

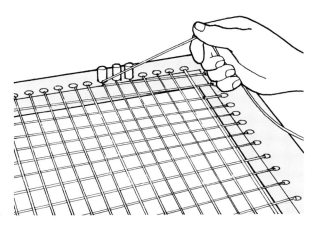

The second set of horizontals are woven **under** and then **over** the vertical pieces (Step 4). As for the first horizontals, peg one end of the cane with the shiny side up. Thread the cane under the first verticals and pull up through the two vertical strands, then over the second verticals. Repeat with each pair of verticals. Work from side to side towards the back of the seat. Occasionally run the cane through your fingers to check that it is not twisting. Do not worry if the weave looks a little untidy as the diagonals will square it up.

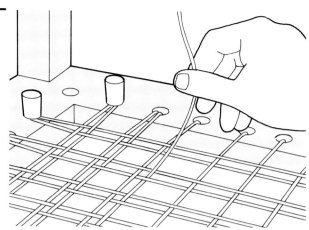

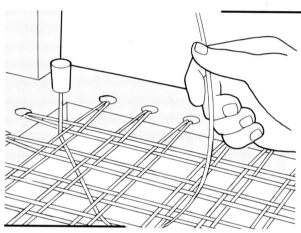

Start weaving the diagonals at the back left hand corner of the seat (Step 5). Peg the hole and insert the cane, shiny side up, **over** the first pair of horizontals and then **under** the first pair of verticals. Moving towards the lower right hand corner, continue weaving **over** the horizontals and **under** the verticals.

Try to keep the cane straight as you weave the diagonals. You should pull it tight every six inches (15 centimetres) or so. As you pull the cane through, the whole weave will tighten and begin to look like the finished product, but be careful that the cane does not break when in flattens into the intersection. When weaving diagonals you should proceed with patience and care, concentrating as you go. Remember that the only way to correct errors is to unweave all that you have already done.

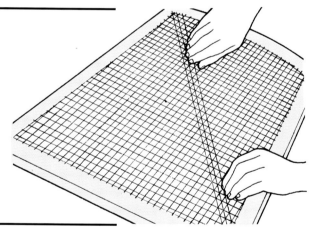

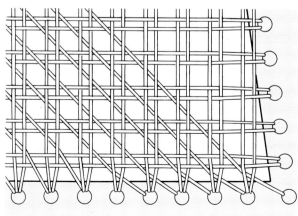

If the seat is not perfectly square, the diagonals, when pulled tight, will not hit the opposite corner exactly, since the strands will be at an angle of 45°. Peg the cane into the nearest available hole, missing one if necessary or using the same hole twice. Always use corner holes twice. Bring the cane up through the next hole in the front of the seat to your left, and then weave back to the hole on the left of where you started.

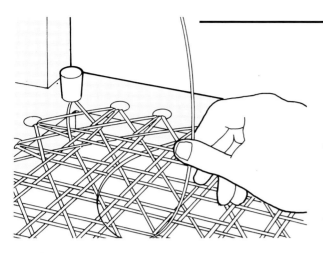

*For the second diagonals (Step 6), you should start in the opposite corner and weave at right angles to the first diagonals. You should use the same corner holes twice. This time the strands pass **under** the horizontals and **over** the verticals.*

To prepare for the beading (Step 7) and achieve a neater finish, gently hammer a peg into every alternate hole (but not the corner holes). Any loose ends in holes that will not be pegged should be poked up into the adjacent one first and held in place while the peg is driven in.

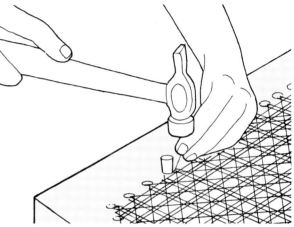

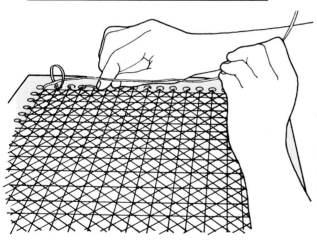

Securing the beading is the final step of the weave. It is usually done with two sizes of cane, numbers two and six. Start by pegging the thinner cane into the back corner hole, leaving about two inches (five centimetres) protruding from the top. Bend this short end down into the next unpegged hole and bring the long end up through the same hole to secure the short end. Then insert the heavier cane length into the corner hole and position it along the holes at the sides of the chair. The thinner cane is then looped over the thick and taken down the same hole.

Once you have successfully completed one caning project using the Seven Step Tradition weave, you will feel confident to try it again not only on chairs but also for screens, panelled doors, bed heads and even square light shades. Remember that you can cane chairs that have never been caned before. This often completely rejuvenates old dining room and sitting room chairs, especially if you also restain and polish them.

To cane a chair which has never been caned before you will have to drill the holes for weaving. They should be drilled all round the frame from top to bottom and should be at exactly the same spacing. To achieve this, measure the overall dimensions of the sides and the back and front. The centre front hole must line up with the centre back hole. If the seat is square this is not so important because you weave the verticals as you would weave the horizontals described in the instructions for the diagram at the bottom of page 52.

The size of the holes you drill will depend on the sizes of the cane you intend using. If you plan to use only grade six for a very strong seat, the holes can be quarter of an inch (six millimetres) in diameter. If you plan to use a variety of cane sizes, the holes should not be larger than an eighth of an inch (three millimetres). They should also be spaced at half inch (one centimetre) intervals.

Project 2

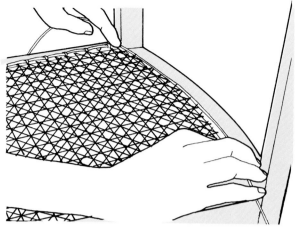

The beading for the curved back of a seat is done with dampened cane. It must be curved by gently bending it round at one inch (two centimetre) intervals until it is the required shape. The thicker cane should be about four inches (10 centimetres) longer than the measurement from corner to corner. This is to give sufficiently long ends to start and finish the beading technique as described previously.

Continue with the beading but just before the corner, bend the thicker cane gently into a mitre and do the same with the next piece of thick cane intended for the front beading. Place them both in the hole and hammer in a peg on the inside of the hole so that the front piece can fold over the peg, thus holding it. Continue using the same piece of thin cane you used for the first side of beading. Continue in this way around the chair until you reach the other back corner hole.

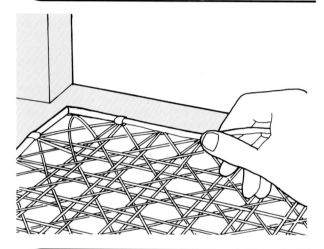

Use a sharp-cutting knife to trim and tidy up the ends on the underside of the seat rails.

Right: The finished chair after it has been revived, polished and recaned. The dark sheen of the newly polished wood complements the attractive light-coloured cane to great effect

Project 2

This chair has badly splayed legs and it needs complete re-upholstering. The woodwork is easily and quickly fixed by cutting false tenons and glueing them in place.

However the major restoration work involves re-upholstering the chair with traditional techniques and materials including horsehair as the main stuffing. Although modern foam rubber can be used, horsehair gives a better, more natural shape if used skilfully. If you intend to upholster an actual antique it is essential that you use horsehair, or some similar fibre, since anything else would reduce the value of the chair. Horsehair is often difficult to obtain and can be expensive. If you cannot get real horsehair, use Algerian fibre. This comes from an Algerian palm tree and is relatively inexpensive. You will need about four or five pounds (two kilograms) of either material for the average-sized dining chair. Algerian fibre needs to be teased out more than horsehair.

The other materials you will need are twine made from flax and hemp for sewing the bridle ties which hold the horsehair in place and for stitching the edges; a ten inch (25 centimetre) straight upholsterer's needle; and a firmly-woven hessian or burlap for covering the webbing. You will need a piece of fabric the area of the base of the seat with enough extra all round for the depth of the padding and for turnings. In addition, a piece of burlap and calico are needed. These should be the same size as the seat area with about seven inches (18 centimetres) extra all round. Wadding is used with the calico to prevent the horsehair from penetrating the main cover. Allow the same amount as for the calico. Braiding is used to cover the tacks which hold the main cover. Buy enough, of the kind with an adhesive backing, to cover all sides of the seat.

You should be able to estimate the amount of webbing you will need from the old webbing on the chair. There are many grades of webbing available. The highest grade is made from pure flax and is a twilled weave, black and white in colour. Another black and white grade is made from jute and cotton, sometimes with linen and hemp threads to give added strength. Plain or striped brown webbing is the cheapest grade.

Springs are sewn onto the webbing with a curved needle. They are also lashed at the top to hold them secure and to give the chair a good, fixed shape. The webbing is placed underneath the frame of the seat if springs are to be used. The springs are placed at the junctions of the webbing. The ends of the springs, where the wire twists are rounded, are turned towards the middle of the seat. This means that when the springs are lashed they will form a dome shape in the centre which is where most of the weight has to be taken.

The springs are then sewn to the webbing from underneath, making three stitches all around the base of the spring, tying a knot at each stitch on the underside. For this step use a curved upholsterer's needle and a long length of twine.

Below: The dining chair ready for the necessary woodwork repairs before the task of upholstering can begin. The old upholstery has been removed. The two front legs are splayed because of broken tenons. These in turn have caused the rails of the seat to become loose

Finish it off by tying the end of the twine to the main length in a slip knot. The lashing is then done to secure the springs to the sides of the seat to prevent them from moving about.

To lash the springs, hammer tacks halfway into the rails of the seat, one opposite each spring. Cut lengths of laid cord twice the width of the seat. Leaving a tail of cord which will stretch to the top of the nearest spring, tie the cord round the tack at the back of the seat. Hammer the tack into the seat rail. Take the main length of cord to the nearest spring towards the front of the chair and wind it round the second from top coil. Thread it through to the other side of the same spring, this time winding round the top coil.

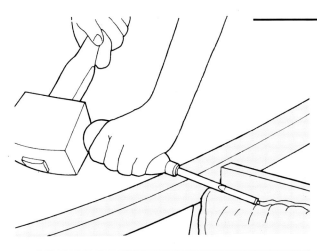

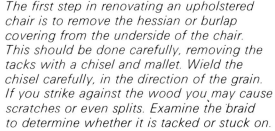

The first step in renovating an upholstered chair is to remove the hessian or burlap covering from the underside of the chair. This should be done carefully, removing the tacks with a chisel and mallet. Wield the chisel carefully, in the direction of the grain. If you strike against the wood you may cause scratches or even splits. Examine the braid to determine whether it is tacked or stuck on.

Remove all the tacks holding the top and inner covers and the thin second layer of stuffing. Cut through the stitches round the edges of the seat, remove all tacks and lift off the cloth exposing the horsehair. Cut the loose stitching holding the horsehair in place. If you wash and dry the horsehair, it regains its original 'buoyancy' and can be used again. Next extract all the tacks holding down the first cover of hessian or burlap, exposing the webbing. It is best to replace the webbing.

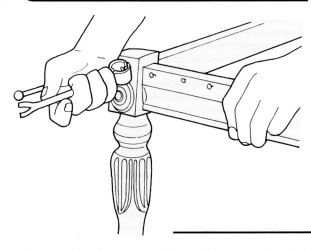

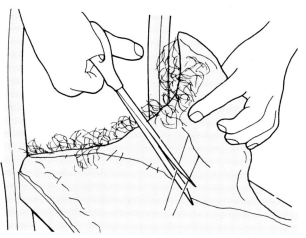

Particular care should be taken when removing the tacks. Try to lever the tacks, if you have to do so, parallel with the side rails of the seat, and then remove them with pincers. Also use pincers to take out any remaining tacks when all the upholstery has been removed. If any tacks are difficult to extract, it is best to hammer them home using a light cabriole hammer. Clean the frame and fill all the holes with a plastic woodfiller.

Proceed to the next spring in the row and wind the cord round the top coil and then thread it through the same spring to wind it round the second from top coil. Tie it tightly around the tack at the front of the chair.

Now take the tail of cord at each tack to the nearest spring and tie it to the top coil on the side nearest to the tack. Pull it tightly so that the spring leans towards the frame of the seat. Repeat this for the other springs, keeping the cord parallel to the first length. Repeat again with two lengths of cord running across the chair.

The first layer of hessian or burlap should be stitched to the springs in the same way they were attached to the webbing. Make a knot at each stitch to keep it in place. A curved needle will make this stitching much easier.

Whether you are using springs or not, it is important to keep the stuffing even during each stage of upholstering. Stuffing can easily be knocked out of shape, while tacking one of the covers for example, or while you are starting to top stitch. You can even this out using a tool called a regulator. This has a sharp end which you insert under the fabric to guide the stuffing into a good shape. Feel the stuffing with your hands as you are working and, whenever necessary, use the regulator to make adjustments. The additional bother makes the difference between a well-finished and a poor job.

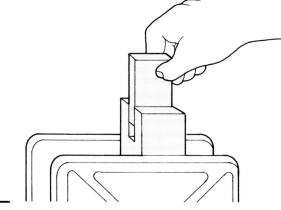

Repair the broken tenons using a restoration device known as a false tenon. First remove the front legs and the side rails. After removing the jagged, old tenon, place the rail in a vice and cut a mortise to a depth of about two inches (five centimetres). Gauge the depth of the old mortise in the leg and add this measurement to the two inches. This is the length of the new false tenon. Saw the tenon using suitable wood and glue it into the new mortise in the rail.

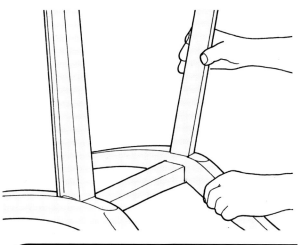

After making two false tenons, glue them into the old mortises in the legs. Refit the rails to the chair, again by gluing, and sash clamp until the glue has dried.

To strengthen the chair, screw wood blocks into the corners; as demonstrated on the right. You can measure for these by marking with a pencil about three inches (seven centimetres) down the rails from each corner. Measure the diagonal across the rails for the third side of the triangle. Make four blocks and then glue them into position. Screw them to the rails taking care not to penetrate the front of the rails. The wood blocks are then water stained and the whole chair revived with wax and french polish.

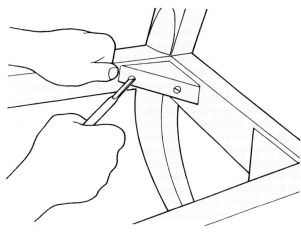

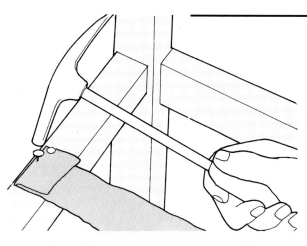

If the chair is to have no springs, the webbing is attached to the upper side of the seat. Start with the centre strand of webbing on the back rail. Without cutting from the roll, fold the webbing over by about one inch (two centimetres). Place it in position on the back rail about half an inch (one centimetre) in from the edge with the folded piece on top. Tack it in place, hammering three five eighth inch (15 millimetres) improved tacks in a row. Place a second row of two tacks near the inner edge.

Standing at the front of the chair, make a loop in the webbing and place it, from underneath, in the slot in the webbing strainer. Hold it in place on top with the peg. Strain the webbing by pulling the handle towards you. Place the webbing in position on the front rail and pull it tightly. Tack it down on the single thickness, using three improved tacks placed in a row. Remove the webbing from the strainer and cut it about one inch (two centimetres) from the tacks. Fold the excess over and hammer in two more tacks.

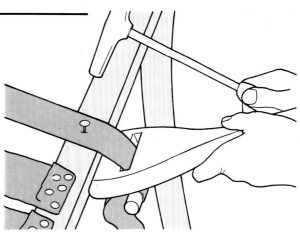

Insert the remaining lengths of webbing in the same number and position as on the original upholstery, using the strainer to achieve maximum tautness. Interweave the cross strands as you go.

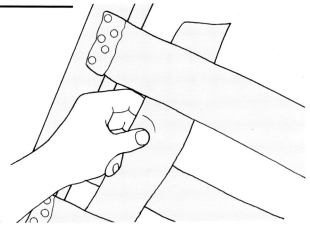

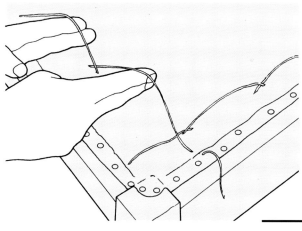

Cut a piece of hessian or burlap to cover the seat, allowing a turning all round. Place this along the back rail and fold the excess so that it is uppermost. Tack at one inch (two centimetre) intervals. Cut to fit, round the back uprights if necessary. Pull to the front edge keeping the grain of the material straight and tack through a single thickness. Fold up the turning and tack down. Attach the third edge as the back and the fourth as the front, folding the cloth parallel to the edge of the frame. Now sew the bridle ties onto the hessian.

Tease out a handful of the horsehair stuffing, removing all lumpy pieces, and place it under the first bridle. Do this for all the bridles and then fill the middle with more horsehair so that there is a loose, dome-shape of horsehair in the centre of the chair which is about two inches (five centimetres) high around the edges.

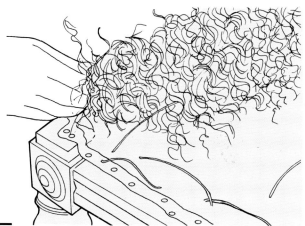

Stuffing should be placed correctly in the first instance. The stuffing is tucked under bridle ties. To do these, thread a spring needle with enough twine to go twice round the sides of the seat. Start with a stitch in the hessian or burlap one inch (two centimetres) long and one inch from the edge. Pull it through, leaving a four inch (ten centimetre) tail. Tie the main length of the twine to the tail in a slip knot. Insert the needle about four inches away, pointing it back toward the slip stitch. Pull it out about three inches (seven centimetres) from the starting point. You should then have a stitch loose enough so that you can insert two fingers underneath it without stressing the twine. This will allow enough space for the horsehair.

Continue making the ties around the edges of the seat making sure that a one inch (two centimetre) stitch is placed at each corner, adjusting the length of the bridles if necessary. The horsehair is then placed under these bridles, after it has been teased out to remove lumps. Allow some horsehair to overhang the edges by a small amount. This should be the same all round.

At first sight, upholstery seems a complicated art, requiring a great deal of knowledge. But with patience and attention to detail, it is a skill you can acquire. Even with your first project you can achieve a degree of success which will surprise you. You should take your time at every step, study and re-read the instructions carefully.

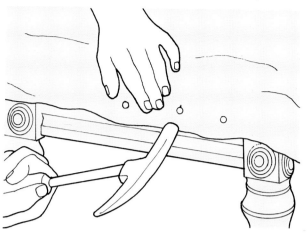

Cut a piece of lightweight hessian or burlap. to cover the stuffing. Position it carefully over the horsehair and tack it in the middle on each side. Do not drive the tacks all the way in. This is called temporary tacking. When the hessian or burlap is centrally placed and you are satisfied that it is straight, you can insert a few more tacks. Place these at two inch (five centimetre) intervals to secure the material for panel stitching.

Remove the temporary tacking and tuck the edge of the hessian or burlap under the horsehair. Secure it to the edges with tacks. Thread an upholsterer's needle with a length of twine. Insert the unthreaded point at an angle of 45° just above the tacks and about two inches (five centimetres) from the corner. When the eye appears stop and push the needle back into the stuffing, to emerge one inch (two centimetres) closer to the corner. Pull the twine through leaving a three inch (seven centimetre) tail and tie this to the main twine length in a slip knot.

Pull this stitching tight so that the stuffing is shifted towards the edge. Reinsert the needle one inch (two centimetres) to the right, just short of the second stitch. Before withdrawing the needle, wind the twine around it and pull tightly. Repeat the same stitch at two inch (five centimetre) intervals right around the seat.

Continue this stitch all around the edges so that there is a fat roll of horsehair with a cavity in the middle of the seat. Make some more bridle ties in the cavity, and fill it with horsehair to make a dome shape.

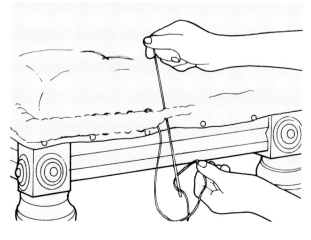

Cover the chair with a piece of calico.
Temporary tack it with three eighth inch
(nine millimetre) fine tacks to the seat
frame. The tacks should be clear of the
polished wood. The calico can fit around
the back uprights of the chair if you fold it
back diagonally and cut from the corner to
the fold. Take each piece round the upright,
fold it under and cut away the excess. If the
chair has rounded front corners, fold the
excess fabric into a double or inverted pleat.
If square, a single pleat is sufficient as
shown below.

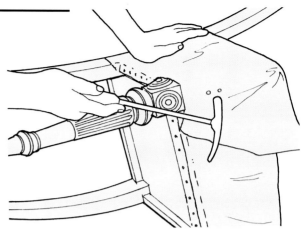

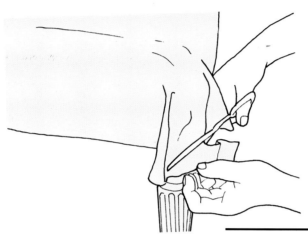

Cover the calico with wadding to prevent
the horsehair coming through. Cut the cover
fabric, allowing about two inches (five
centimetres) more than the original fabric.
Temporary tack it in place. Finish the corners
as for the calico.

Tack down the cover along the edge of the
show-wood or underneath the seat,
depending on the type of chair. If the cover
is finally tacked on the underneath of the
seat, you should cover the entire bottom of
the seat with black hessian or burlap,
folded under for tidiness.

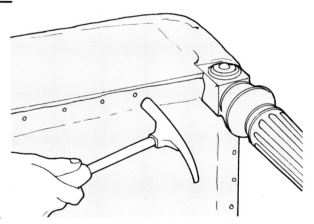

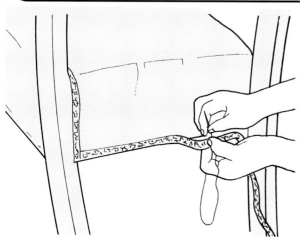

If the cover is tacked along the line of show-
wood, as on the finished chair on the right,
you should finish off by hiding the tacks and
raw edges with a suitable braid. Most braids
can now be bought backed with a latex
adhesive and are easy to apply. Mitre the
corners of the braid.

Project 3: A Gate-Leg Table

A gate-leg table is given a new lease of life. Its loose framework is strengthened, the damaged gate sections are restored and a broken leaf is repaired

Left: The gate-leg table before restoration, with the gate broken away from the main frame. Two rails are missing, one from the rail and the other from the gate. The swivel dowels are also smashed. The main task lies in replacing the missing section of the leaf which is broken at the joint

Gate-leg tables are one of the most attractive and pleasing pieces of furniture. Despite its broken top, loose framework and damaged gate sections this one is no exception. The tightening of the whole structure is a routine part of restoration work but the repair to the broken leaf is a major job. The leaves of such tables are frequently broken. But such fractures are usually small and often only involve damage to the moulding. The two sections can either be rub jointed, as described in this project, or centre pinned with dowels. Four dowels should be used and they can be placed by scratch-gauging the centre thickness of the table edge. Then the two sections are placed face to face and the dowel positions marked with a square. Place the gauge along these positions and mark the centre of the dowel holes. Drill out the holes and glue the dowels into place. Then assemble and clamp. Remember to place two pieces of wood under the feet of the sash clamp so as not to damage the piece of furniture.

You can find the positions of the dowel holes using a slightly less orthodox approach. Hammer some pins along the face of one of the sections, after first cutting off the heads of the pins. Now press the old and new sections together. The impression made by the pins will give you the positions of the dowels. The pins should be removed before you drill.

If the fracture is quite small, the repair is still carried out in the same way. Rub jointing will probably not be needed and you will only have to use one or two dowels.

The rule joint (a series of three hinges which attach the leaves to the table top) on this table is in good working order but on some gate-leg tables it can be unreliable, usually because of swelling of the timber due to dampness. The leaf and the top are usually rule-jointed and held apart by a metal hinge. Swelling will cause the joint to bend so that the leaf does not lower correctly, although it is satisfactory in the raised position.

The best way to deal with this problem is to unscrew the hinges and allow the separated parts of the joint to dry out in a warm room. Remove the polish and varnish with a piece of sandpaper to speed up the drying process.

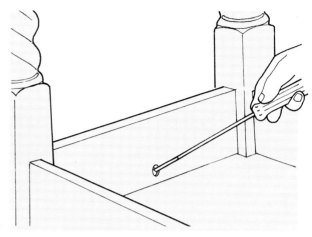

The leaves of gate-leg tables are attached in a variety of ways, the most common on older tables is the rule joint, a series of three hinges countersunk on the opposite side to the joint. Each of these is held by four screws, which should be removed. The fixed part of the top is usually screwed to the cradle by up to six screws, recessed and inserted diagonally. These must be unscrewed.

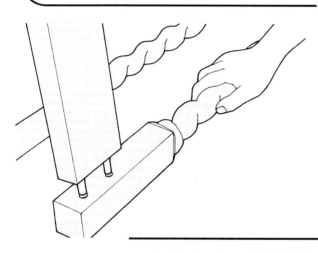

After unscrewing all sections of the table, reglue joints which have become loose. The gates are attached to the main frame by strong dowels which allow them to swivel. When these are broken, the old dowels should be removed by drilling with an electric drill or brace and bit. New dowels are then fitted after being measured and glued into place.

Now fit the gates into the framework of the table, making sure the assembly is square by using a try square.

If you have to replace any of the hinges, it is important that the hinge is embedded directly beneath the top of the moulded part of the joint. If this is not done correctly the leaf will become stuck when it is lowered and raised. Buy a hinge similar in type and size to the one you are replacing and screw it into place with the leaf in the lowered position. Smear wax or candle grease on the hinges to prevent stiffness and give a smoother action.

The gate sections of this kind of table also present problems. Swivelled on dowels, the gate folds snugly into the main frame by means of two housings, one in the leg of the gate, the other in the lower rail of the frame. The housing at the foot of the gate leg goes to a depth of half its thickness and a violent knock or a heavy weight placed on top of it, during removals for example, can cause a break.

You can repair this by cutting a piece of wood of the same dimensions as the part of the foot which formed the housing. Glue and dowel this into the top of the foot and then into the lower part of the leg.

The stop strip on the underneath of the leaves is often broken or knocked out of place because

Left: Removing broken pieces of dowel. Dowelling is used in most gate-leg tables to enable the gates to swivel from the main frame

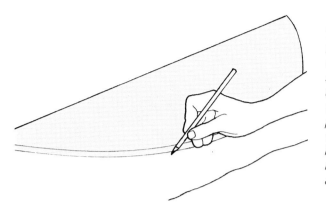

To repair the broken section of the damaged leaf, you will need a template. The first template is made by placing a sheet of strong paper on top of the complete, undamaged leaf and tracing its edge. This way of doing it prevents the paper from puckering if the leaf is accidentally pushed with the hand. But for the inexperienced, it is probably best to insert the paper underneath the leaf as shown in the diagram. Use a heavy pencil to get a firm clear line.

When the template is marked and cut, it is transferred to the broken section of leaf. A straight edge is used to mark the new section needed. It is again important to make sure that the template and the straight edge do not slide as you are marking. Press down on the straight edge and make sure there are no creases in the paper large enough to give you a distorted measurement, which could result in wasting a piece of valuable wood.

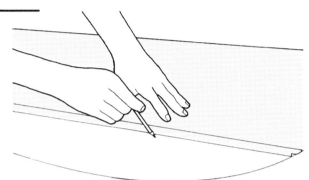

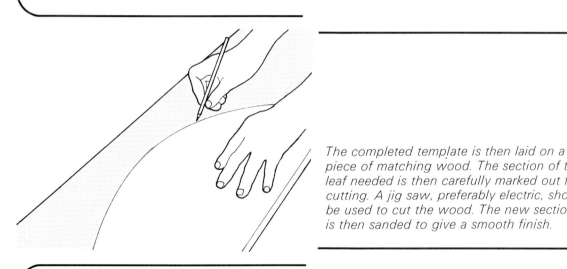

The completed template is then laid on a piece of matching wood. The section of the leaf needed is then carefully marked out for cutting. A jig saw, preferably electric, should be used to cut the wood. The new section is then sanded to give a smooth finish.

The new section of leaf is jointed to the old section by rub jointing. First place the old section tightly in a vice. The edges of both pieces to be joined are then glued. The new section is rubbed backwards and forwards along the edge of the old, not more than two inches (five centimetres) at a time. Both sections are kept level using the thumbs on one side and the forefingers on the other. The object is to create a vacuum between the two sections. When this occurs the joint sticks and great force will be needed to break it.

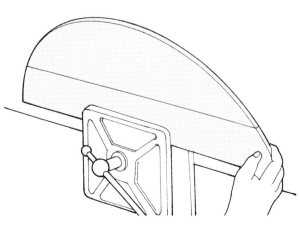

When the glue has dried, the new section is moulded with a spokeshave. The new wood is gradually rounded to match the shape of the edge of the old part of the leaf. The shaving should begin where the old and new sections are jointed. On this table the moulding has a vertical edge on the top and so the centre of the circumference of the rounded part of the moulding is lower than at first appears. This kind of moulding can also be done using a special tool called a moulding plane.

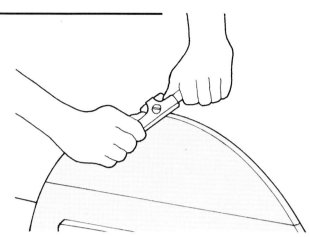

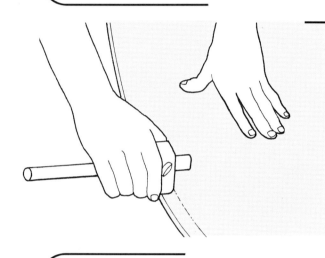

The vertical dip in the top of the moulding is marked out using a gauge. The depth of the dip is first gauged from the old section of the leaf.

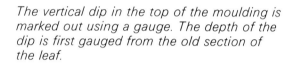

The dip is then cut with a chisel. A sharp bevel-edged chisel should be used and held parallel to the side of the table. When this is completed, sand the new section to a smooth finish.

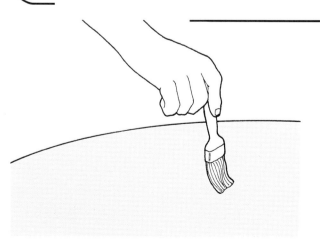

The new section of the leaf is stained to match the rest of the table and polished. After this has been done, revive the whole of the table, starting at the top, before wax polishing as a final finish.

the nails have rusted. It is best to glue these back into place. When you remove the broken pieces, an impression of the strip will be left so that there should be no difficulty in refitting a new piece of wood. Copy the dimensions of the old strip. To achieve an attractive finish you can taper the strips to about 45° so that the square edge does not knock anybody's knee when they are sitting at the table. Do not forget to water stain the new strips.

Finally if the top is warped you can clamp it to another flat surface after removing it from the frame. To avoid damage and to gain extra leverage, place a long batten under the soles of the clamps which should be placed at each corner of the top.

Above: The gleaming table with all the restoration work completed. Besides the making of the template and the cutting of the moulding of the new section of leaf, most of the damage is easily corrected

Project 4: A Chest of Drawers

A very worn and badly damaged, though still attractive, chest of drawers can be completely rejuvenated with the repair of drawer runners, replacement of fittings and knobs, and the reconstruction of the chest's back

Left: The badly-damaged chest of drawers–– one drawer is broken, the back is missing and most of the bottom has been gutted by dry rot. But the spare drawer means that a creative restoration can be carried out. This involves making a template so that specially shaped pieces can be cut for the bottom of the front

This chest of drawers is in bad shape. The back is missing, the bottom is badly damaged by dry rot, one of the drawers is broken, and a knob is missing. In fact, the piece would probably be irredeemable except that there is a spare drawer which came with the chest. This drawer will provide the material for the necessary restoration work. By cutting the sides of the chest to form the two halves of bracket feet, you can then complete these feet and design a template from the front wood of the spare drawer.

The back of the chest is missing. Its replacement will not simply involve measuring and glueing the necessary amount of wood to make a square-shaped back, it will instead incorporate a shaped end which completes the bracket feet at the back of the chest.

Half of the four bracket feet are shaped from the overlap of the sides of the chest. These protrude beneath the bottom drawer by about five inches (twelve centimetres). These protruding sides are cut, after marking, in a trapezoid shape with sides jutting inwards by about 20 degrees. The slanted bracket feet are made up from the designed front and the new back.

Chips and dents in veneer, as on the front of the chest, usually present little problem. Their treatment depends upon the grain of the veneer. Curled, swirled grains should be matched if possible. The jagged edges should be cut back with a knife or chisel to give a straighter edge so that it will be easier to measure and insert the new piece. The waste should be carefully removed, taking care not to damage the new edge.

Broken knobs can be bought from a shop or, if this is not possible, you can have them specially turned. On most chests of drawers, knobs are fixed by boring through the drawer front and then glueing the knob into place. If a broken knob is tightly glued, take care when you remove it not to damage the adjoining surface, especially if veneered. The shoulder of the knob should be gently chipped away with a chisel. It should then be possible to tap out the dowelled part of the knob from the inside of the drawer.

Sometimes the rusted screws of metal knobs and handles enlarge the screw holes. When the knobs and handles are replaced the holes should be filled with wood plugs so that the new screws will grip. It may be advisable to drill new holes close to the old filled holes. Check that your fittings will cover the repair before drilling.

Most faults on chests are in the drawers. The drawer is a moving part and wear is inevitable, particularly as chests are often filled beyond their capacity. The damage usually includes broken and split bottoms, worn runner rails, loose joints, worn sides, split knobs and, on some drawers, damaged cocked beads.

There is really only one way of dealing with loose joints––take them apart and re-glue. Any screws or nails should be removed from the bottom. The sides should be separated from the front and back by knocking them outwards with a hammer and a flat piece of wood, if the joints are very loose, or by hitting them with a mallet. This is an extra precaution because a piece of wood inserted between the mallet and the drawer helps to avoid bruises or splits which may warrant a new side.

All the old glue should be thoroughly removed from the joints. If you use a chisel to do this, be careful not to gash the wood. If the joint is obstinate, it may be necessary to soften the glue with a little hot water. Too much water could cause swelling. The dovetails should be perfectly dry before re-glueing after which the joint should be re-assembled in the same manner as it was taken apart, with a mallet or hammer and wood. Wipe away the surplus glue with a rag. If the joints are actually worn from use you can mix fine sawdust to the glue to give added substance.

Sides are sometimes worn along the top edges. Most of the wear will be at the back of the drawer because drawers are sometimes left half open. The most effective way of dealing with worn sides, particularly if the wear goes down into the groove which holds the bottom in place, is to level off the edge and fit a new piece right along the length of the edge. Glueing a new piece should not present problems if the repair does not sink into the groove. If the wear is in the groove, make a small rebate with a rebate plane. In both cases, glue to the side edges only, not the bottom.

After removing all broken sections of the chest bottom, measure to replace it from the inside edge of the front rails to the edge of the back, and then along the length of the back, from the outside edges on both sides. When cut and sanded, glue blocks along the sides of the piece and then glue and fit them into position under the runners of the bottom drawer.

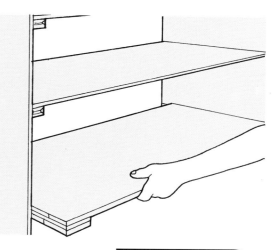

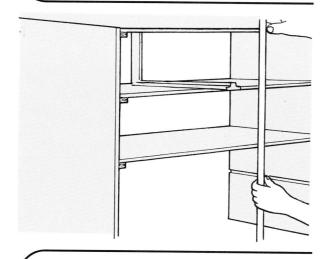

The length of the boards for the new back is measured from under the top of the chest to the lower edge of the glued blocks holding the bottom in place. The piece is then measured for width. The two end boards should extend, after the first cutting, right to the bottom of the chest. Cut them to form plain bracket-type feet. All the boards should be glued along their edges and then screwed to the carcass. To match the feet at the back, cut the sides of the chest to form plain bracket feet.

Check the end boards of the back to make sure they fit well, particularly the bracket feet. The uncut board, extending to the bottom of the chest, should be placed in position and a line drawn across at the lower edge of the new bottom. To determine the angle of the bracket feet, draw another line from the bottom of the board to meet the first line at an angle of about 20°. The side feet should be measured in a similar way.

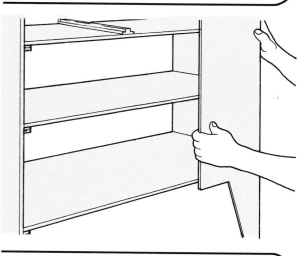

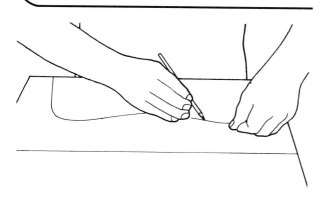

If you decide to use a spare drawer to form a moulded front for the exposed bottom of the cabinet, a template has to be designed first. Here it is designed freestyle, but if faced with a similar problem you can get ideas for your template from furniture catalogues and books. Draw your design on a piece of cardboard and cut out with a sharp knife. A template should also be designed for the sides to give a shape to the bracket feet.

Drawer bottoms are invariably made of two pieces of wood jointed in the middle. It is a common fault for this joint to break and sag under continuous weight. Both edges of the joint should be very lightly planed and then glued together again. To make the repaired joint straight, it will be necessary to place the two pieces of wood, after glueing, on a flat surface and weigh them down while the glue is drying. Place the weights at the ends, especially if the pieces of wood are bowed upwards. Remember that excess glue will spill from the bottom of the wood so that the flat surface on which you work should be protected by newspaper. A strip of canvas can be glued along the repaired joint if the drawer takes heavy items. Strips of canvas can also be used to cover small split ends.

Cocked beads are pieces of moulding glued along the edges of the sides, front and back of a drawer to protect the veneer. For this reason, they are frequently damaged. In some cases the whole length of beading has been damaged. In most cases, however, the damage is confined to small pieces that have broken off. Along the bottom and sides of the drawer the dovetails are made so as to allow a rebate to be inserted for the beads. The beading round the front of the top of the drawer is usually mitred. You can make these cocked beads up yourself by cutting a strip from an old piece of matching wood. Cut the beads to the width of the rebate which is already cut in the drawer.

Sometimes the front of a drawer is made from a solid piece of wood surrounded by a moulding which overlaps and stands proud of the carcass of the drawer. Often the corners of this moulding are damaged. Repairs entail glueing a section of similar wood into place, using a mitred joint if necessary. Instructions on how to use a mitre box are on page 80.

One of the first things you should check on drawers is whether the stops need repairing. Drawer stops are small pieces of wood, about one inch square (two centimetres), glued onto the rail just underneath the front of the drawer. Sometimes they consist only of dowels glued into the rail to protrude on top by about half an inch (one centimetre).

By removing the drawer the position of the stops should be obvious. If the piece of furniture is old and the drawers have been opened many times, the stops may have scraped, and therefore damaged, the back of the underneath of the drawer. If the sides and bottom of the drawer are repaired, the stops will not cause this problem. But it is wise to take the added precaution of placing the new stops in a slightly different position. The front of the stop should be placed against the inside edge of the front of the drawer. This can be gauged to the thickness of the front and then marked on the rail. The new stop should then be fixed with glue and pinned. The pins should be punched just below the surface to prevent the heads catching the drawer bottom. The grain of the stops should run from back to front. End grain wears better.

The usual damage to drawer rails (those attached to the carcass) is when they slightly curve in the centre, causing trouble to two drawers at once. The most effective remedy is to replace the rail completely. These rails are usually cut from a piece of pine and they act as a guide for the drawers to run on. Measure up for the new rail by noting the mark left by the old one. If you wish to correct this problem without cutting a new rail the following remedy can be tried. Chisel a dovetail about six inches (15 centimetres) wide into the rail, into which is glued a wedge of wood of comparable length. While the glue is drying, use a temporary wedge to prop up the sagging rail. This should be slightly overlength, by about quarter of an inch (six millimetres). When the glued repair has dried, remove this prop. This should cure the curvature if the rail is not too much out of alignment. The effectiveness of the repair depends on the degree of sag and the width of the dovetail. If the sag is very pronounced, the dovetail should be as wide as possible. It is possible to experiment as the repair is being carried out. If the first dovetail does not correct the curvature, remove the wedge and start again, this time using a wedge two inches (five centimetres) wider. Continue until you achieve the right width. Remember to keep the repair clean of glue each time you try this.

When the template designs have been marked onto the front of the spare drawer and the sides of the cabinet, cut the shapes out using a pad saw. (An electric jig saw can do this much faster and, for the amateur, with greater accuracy.) Sand the pieces to smoothness.

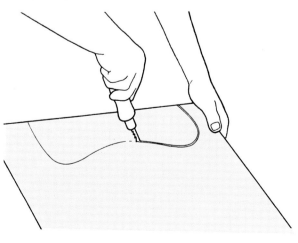

*Above: Hammering pins into the piece
shaped from a template. If a spare drawer is
not available with the chest of drawers you
set out to restore, it may be possible to buy
old, matching wood, or even to buy another
old chest which is clearly beyond
redemption and likely therefore to be cheap*

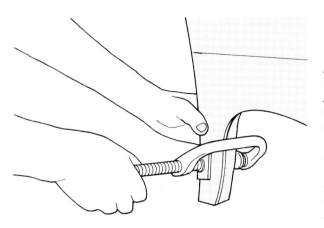

The designed front piece is then glued and pinned into place. Put wooden strengtheners behind the junction of the front and side parts of the bracket feet. Such strengtheners can be quite roughly shaped but should be small enough so that they are not visible when viewed from the front. Glue them to both sides of the bracket feet and clamp with a G clamp until the glue has dried. To make up the length of the designed front, cut a small rectangular piece of wood and glue it into place.

Stain the back of the cabinet and all new surfaces to match the colour of the chest, using a brush. A smaller artist's brush can be used for touching in the stains to any veneer which might show exposed wood. The undersides, bracket strengtheners, and edges of the designed pieces should also be coloured to match.

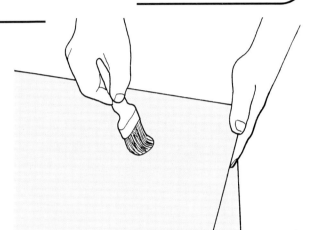

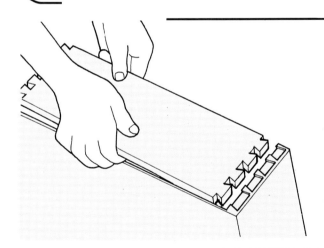

To mend the drawer, first take it apart by gently knocking the dovetails out with a wooden mallet. You should approach using the mallet with great care. Take your time and tap from the inside of the drawer. Clean the dovetails of all residue glue, then reglue and rejoin as much as possible by force of thumb.

Now tap the dovetails into place using a light hammer. This also forces out much of the excess glue which should be wiped off with a rag or it will dry in lumps and look very unsightly. The drawer should be gripped with a sash clamp while the glue is drying.

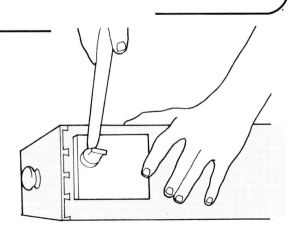

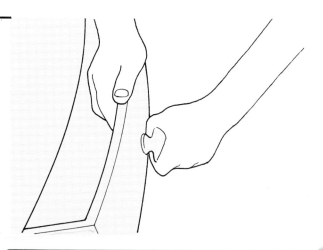

A missing knob can be replaced either by making one yourself or by buying one to match. To make one you will need a lathe. The knobs for this kind of chest are held in place either by a small length of dowel or shaped wood glued in position, or by an open bolt with screw and washer.

A prominent feature of many old chests of drawers are locks, and they are frequently damaged in some way. A common fault is for the screws to have come loose. The simplest remedy for this, if the thickness of the wood allows, is to use longer screws of the same diameter. Another easy remedy is to fill the holes with wood plugs thus giving new thread to the screws. If however the screw holes are very distorted, a more complicated repair will have to be carried out.

This is done by cutting small pieces of wood tapered to fit the old screw holes. Shape these with a chisel or knife and glue and tap them into position with a hammer. When the glue has dried, use a sharp chisel to trim the new plug flush with the level of the frame. This should then be sanded. New screw holes can be started with a bradawl or any pointed tool. Since old-type brass screws are fragile and can break when being driven into new wood, use a steel screw in all the holes to prepare the threads for the brass screws.

If you have to remove a lock, you should do so very carefully. Avoid damaging the screws or scratching the surface. The most common internal fault found with locks is a broken or loose spring. If you want to use the old locks again, you can get the spring repaired at a locksmith.

Splits around lock mortises can sometimes be repaired by re-glueing a piece which has still not completely broken off or by replacing it with a new piece. If a new mortise has to be cut into the new wood, it can be marked by smearing the bolt with dark oil and then opening the bolt until a mark is made on the rail. This mark should be the centre of the new mortise.

The designed front piece is cut from the spare drawer and as there is not enough wood, it does not meet in the middle. To cover this gap, square off the ends and cut a small rectangular piece of the same wood. Plane the rectangle to shape and surround it with a cocked bead. Then glue and pin into place. To do this it is necessary to apply glue blocks to the underside of the carcass and the back of the designed section.

For all the variety and number of repairs, a renovated chest of drawers not only looks good but is likely to last you for a long time.

Below: The finished restoration has brought about a complete transformation to the chest of drawers. What had seemed irreparable because of the extent of the damage, particularly to the bottom, has provided an attractive piece of bedroom furniture

Project 5: A Glass-Fronted Cabinet

The restoration of a glass-fronted cabinet can involve many different tasks. This cabinet will have its doors refitted, its top reblocked, and the plinth and cornice moulding restored

The work on the glass-fronted cabinet falls into two categories, that for the top of the cupboard and that for the bottom. On the top, the cornice moulding is badly broken and the moulding on the door has worked loose. The bottom needs more repairs, the most important of which is the work on the plinth. The drawer runners are worn away and the doors require refitting. There are missing sections of veneer on the main body of the carcass.

All the metal fittings on both top and bottom need to be cleaned and put back in place after stripping, staining and polishing the whole cupboard.

Before starting work, the two parts of the cupboard must be separated by unscrewing a sunken screw which is inserted through the base of the top into the top of the bottom.

Cornice moulding is usually fitted to the tops of cupboards and wardrobes by attaching it to blocks glued and nailed on to the top. There are usually about six of these blocks and the moulding is glued and pinned into them.

Besides replacing the moulding on this cabinet, it is necessary to reblock the top of the cupboard. When this is done, mitre the new moulding and fit it into position. Mitring, in this case cutting angles of 45° at both ends of a length of wood, is a simple task if a mitre box is used. It is imperative to make the mitres well so that they fit into each other tightly without gaps which will show both glue and pins.

Cornice and any other mouldings that are applied or worked on the tops and edges of pieces of furniture often become damaged. This is because they project from the main surface. When the damage is in the length of the moulding and not at one of the corners, a local repair will usually suffice. Two angled cuts are made and the damaged piece removed with a chisel. A new matching piece is cut to correspond with the angles already made. This is then glued into place and allowed to dry overnight before the piece is shaped with a plane and sandpaper and finished to the contours of the original moulding. Obviously this will only work for the amateur if the moulding is not too decorative and complicated in shape.

There are two basic types of moulding. Stuck moulding is worked into the solid carcass. The type of damage is confined to smashed corners, bruises and deep scratches. Applied moulding is so called because it is glued to the carcass. The most common damage occurs when it becomes loose or when it has gone completely missing. The door moulding on the glass-fronted cabinet is a good example of applied moulding. The shaped edge of the gate-leg table in one of the earlier projects is an example of stuck moulding.

With stuck moulding there is no difficulty involved in repairing it if the damage is small. Again, the damaged section should be removed by making two angled cuts and a new piece glued into place. If the moulding has to take weight, as does the moulding at the edge of a table top, the new section of wood should be dowelled into place as well as being glued. The new piece of wood should then be shaped using a plane or a spokeshave. (This method is described on page 68 in the project on the gate-leg table.)

For the purposes of repair, applied moulding can often be treated as stuck moulding. If the damage is small, the moulding should not be removed. Instead, a new section can be applied in the manner described for stuck moulding. There is usually no need to dowel applied moulding. In most cases, however, applied moulding is loose or has come away from the surface completely. If the moulding has lost some of its original shape, some form of clamping will be needed when you re-glue it back into place. One way of doing this is to bind the piece with string and use a stick or long nail to wind it tightly. An alternative is to turn the piece of furniture upside down or sideways and weigh the moulding down with a heavy object. In some cases conventional clamps can be used.

Right: The untouched glass-fronted cabinet with a loose shelf is repaired by inserting two new supports along the marks of the old. There is also a broken cornice moulding, sections of oak veneer are missing and the plinth requires an additional piece. The whole cabinet is then stained and polished to look like new

Take the cabinet apart by unscrewing the screw which is recessed into the part of the top which lies on the bottom section of the cupboard. On some cupboards there are up to three of these screws. Then remove the doors, keeping a tight grip to prevent the door from falling and being damaged further. This can easily happen if the screws are old and rusted.

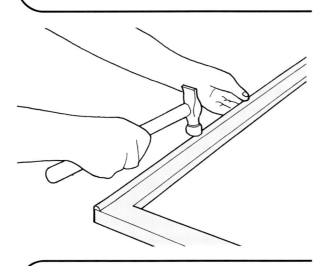

The moulding on doors on this type of cabinet are usually pinned in two or three places as well as being glued. On this cabinet the moulding has worked loose probably because the doors were slammed too often. Fresh glue is all that is needed to repair the damage. All the old glue is scraped away with a chisel.

Cornice moulding usually involves a more complicated type of repair. First measure the length of each piece of moulding required for the sides and the front. Each length is then mitred at the ends to make the corners. This is done simply by inserting the length of moulding into a mitre box and sawing along the 45° opening or groove.

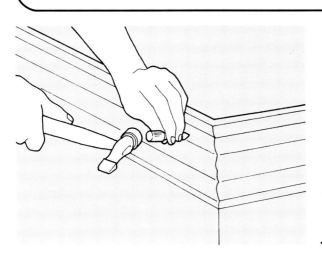

The cornice is then glued into place and the mitres pinned. Using a nail punch, sink the pins so that they do not show. The wax which is used in the staining process later in the project is sufficient to fill these holes.

Below: Mending the shelf which had broken loose. The shelf rests on supports as well as being fitted into scalloped uprights. The insert on the left shows the top of the cupboard after the shelf has been repaired

To repair the damage to the plinth, first cut away a bevelled section beyond the area which has to be dealt with. The important point is to cut the piece as accurately as possible to make fitting a replacement easier, and to give it a more professional finish. You may find that the section you wish to remove is held with pins and glue. Pull the pins with pincers and lever away the glued piece, taking care not to do further damage to any other part of the plinth.

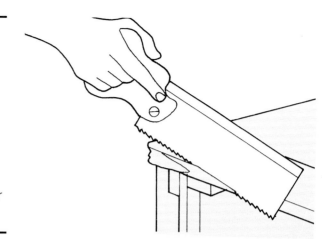

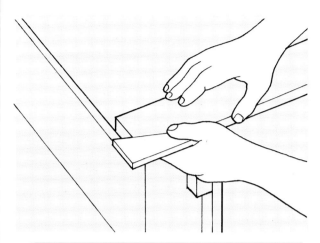

Bevel a new piece of matching wood and shape it to fit into the plinth. This should then be inserted into place, after the area has been sanded and cleaned, using glue and pins. The piece of wood used should be slightly larger than needed so that it overlaps the edges by a small amount.

When the glue has dried, pare the new section of the plinth with a chisel and then plane it to make it level with the rest of the plinth and veneers. Lightly sand the piece with a fine paper and wipe it with a wet cloth in preparation for staining. A wet cloth is used to remove wood dust.

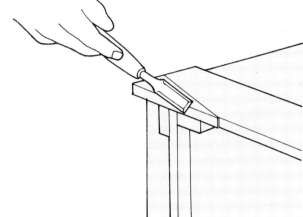

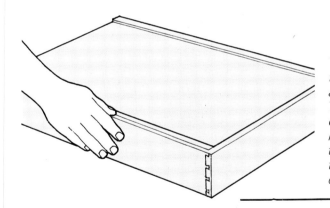

The drawer runners are badly worn and need to be replaced. First measure these up against the length of the side of the drawer. The old runners on the underside of the drawer are already flattened because they have worn down so much. The depth of the runner to be added can be gauged from the good runner. Glue the runners to the drawer.

When the glue has dried, prepare the runner by planing the edges. They should be planed so that the running edge is of a convex shape and will fit snugly into the runner troughs in the rail of the drawer. On the left the repaired drawer is being refitted into the cabinet. The runners need quite a lot of planing and waxing to ensure a frictionless action.

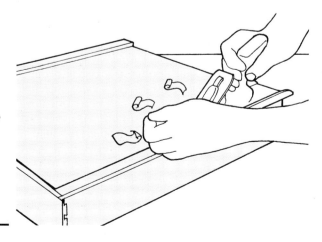

After staining and polishing, clean all the fittings and rescrew them in place when any necessary repairs to the old screw holes have been carried out. In some cases you may find it necessary to replace damaged hardware fittings.

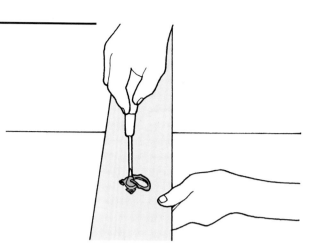

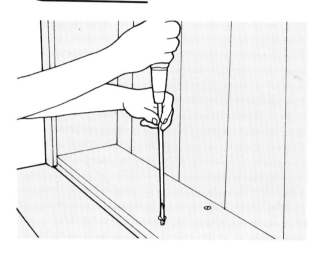

When the restoration work is completed, place the top to the bottom of the cabinet and screw them together. In many old cabinets these screws sometimes rust and work themselves loose, making the insertion holes too large. Plastic woodfiller will remedy this problem. It is then preferable to drill new holes and fit new screws.

Right: The restored cabinet in all its glory. It has been completely repolished and the cleaned handles and fittings greatly enhance the finish. Such cupboards can accommodate a great number of books and they are invaluable for any modern living room

hinges with new hinges which are too thin for the recessed housings. The recesses should be packed with old pieces of veneer or even cardboard so that the hinge is brought level with the side panels of the door.

Compared to refitting the doors, the task of stripping, staining, polishing and waxing the cupboard is a major one. But first remove all the metal parts which are in danger of being smeared with stain. These are usually already stained and need to be cleaned. Metal parts are easily cleaned by immersing them in methylated spirit or de-natured alcohol and then scraping them clean with fine steel wool. There is a danger of scratching so that great care and delicacy is required if you do not wish to irreparably spoil the fitting.

For the task of stripping and staining, follow the procedure described in the pine desk project on pages 40/41. The polish is stripped from top to bottom and the whole surface is then sanded. The cupboard can then be stained to the colour required. All the colours are then levelled up and two coats of polish are applied, rubbing between coats. The piece is then finished with a coat of wax and all the metal parts are refitted.

This type of glass-fronted cabinet is fairly common and you should not have any difficulty in buying one. They are not only spacious but also very attractive whether finished with a light or dark colour or just waxed over the stripped wood in much the same way as the pine desk.

Project 6: A Chaise-Longue

A shabby chaise-longue with one leg and castor missing is presented for restoration. As well as reassembling the carcass of the chaise-longue more solidly, it is beautifully re-upholstered

Left: The chaise-longue just after it was bought. Its battered and dishevelled appearance gives little clue that it will fall apart when the old upholstery is removed. The frame was restored to give a new durability, and provided the preparation for a complete face-lift through upholstery

The chaise-longue in this project was not only shabby and discoloured, it also had one leg and castor missing. When the old upholstery was removed, the whole framework just fell apart, leaving a jumble of seemingly unrelated pieces. When approaching any piece of old upholstered furniture, always dismantle the upholstery carefully. Take detailed notes of every layer, where it was attached to the frame, what stitching was used and keep the old layers of fabric for patterns. The old stuffing can also be washed, dried and, freed from dust, used again.

Before you begin to reassemble the frame, check for woodworm. This should be treated. If you do have to apply woodworm fluid to the carcass, it must be allowed to dry thoroughly or it may spoil the fabric. The tack holes from previous upholstery jobs can be filled with plastic wood and sanded down.

Fortunately this frame was reassembled without too much rebuilding. It is almost always necessary to completely strip old upholstered furniture as the fabric is usually dusty and old, as is the stuffing. At this stage the frame can be strengthened and rejuvenated so that the upholstery work is not wasted. The frame of this chaise-longue had been jointed with dowels glued into place. Many of these had broken or just come out of place so that the major task was to remove the broken dowel ends and replace them with new dowel lengths of the same size and diameter.

The jagged dowels are sawed flush with the rails and then removed, using a brace and bit. The bit should be of the same diameter as the dowels so that the holes are cleaned out perfectly by the drilling.

When this is done new dowels are glued into position and allowed to dry. Then the sub-frames are assembled. The two ends should be assembled first before adding the two main long rails and the back. These sub-frames are glued into each other using the same dowelled jointing. Triangular blocks should then be inserted by screwing into the corners of the seat section to give added strength. This strengthening is essential as people so often sit on the backs and arms of chairs and sofas.

Old dowels are most effectively removed by using a brace and bit of appropriate diameter. If the bit has the same diameter as the dowel, a clean hole will be made so that even the old glue is removed. If the dowel has a jagged end protruding from the holes, it is best to saw this off flush with the rail of the chair.

Dowel joints are simple to remake. Glue back into position dowels of the same diameter and length. All the joints on this chaise-longue are dowelled so that reconstruction is a simple affair. Both of the ends are assembled first. The new dowels are glued into place and a sash clamp is used to reinforce the joint while the glue dries. When the ends have been assembled, the long rails are put into position. The back is then assembled and clamped into position. All corners are strengthened by screwing in triangular blocks.

Replace the missing leg by taking a template from one of the existing legs. Transfer this to a block of matching wood and mark the outline with a pencil. Cut the shape out with a jig saw or a band saw. The template need only approximate the final dimensions of the leg.

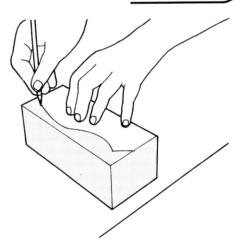

To shape the leg, two tools are used—a shaping plane for the rougher shaping and a spokeshave for cutting the curved parts of the leg and giving a smooth finish. The leg is then stained and polished to match the others after being dowelled into position. Fit the new, matching castor.

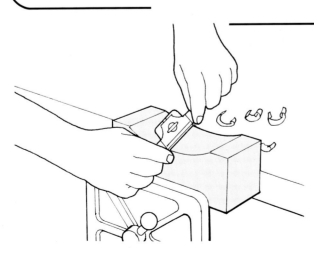

Above: Work on the back of the chaise-longue is begun after first reassembling most of the sub-frames by redowelling the joints. The new leg has been cut, shaped, and placed in position on a new castor

Project 6

Turn the frame upside down and secure the webbing in twin sets along the underneath of the rails. The strips that run from the back to the front are placed first and tacked into position after they have been stretched with a webbing strainer. The same procedure is followed for the long lengths of webbing which extend from the head rail to the foot rail. Weave these in and out of the first set of webbing.

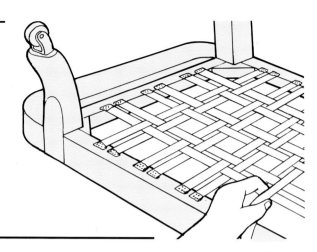

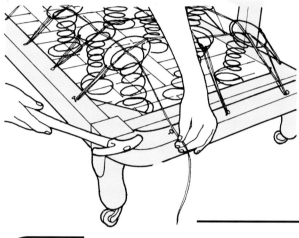

The springs are placed at the junctions of the webbing. They are then attached to the webbing with twine using a curved upholstery needle. To lash the springs, $\frac{5}{8}$ inch (15 millimetre) tacks are half tacked to the frame at the end of each row of springs. The tops of the springs are lashed together and tied to the tacks to compress them and give a fixed position when weight is exerted downwards.

The lashed springs should be covered with heavy hessian or burlap which is tacked along the top face of the rails. Fold and tack it after it has been temporarily fixed and smoothed. Fit it tightly around the uprights, slashing if necessary. The cloth should then be stitched to the springs in the same way that the springs were attached to the webbing.

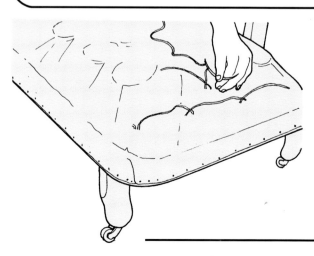

Lay the bridle ties in the hessian (burlap). Details for this are given in the text on page 60. Remember to keep the ties loose enough so that two fingers can rest underneath them.

The next structural repair involves replacing the missing leg. First a template is made from one of the existing legs. The template is placed on a matching piece of wood and marked out. This is then cut out with a jig saw and shaped with a spokeshave and wood file. One castor was found for the stained and polished new leg. If this had not been possible, a whole new set could have been bought and the three existing castors discarded. The frame is now ready for upholstering after the new leg and castor have been dowel-jointed into the rail.

For the upholstery, the frame is first turned upside down to place the webbing. The webbing is the basis for the rest of the upholstery so it is important to position it correctly, tautly and strongly.

Since springs are to be used, the webbing is placed on the underside of the frame. Use the webbing straight from the roll and cut it as you progress with the work. The strips that run from back to front are placed first. The first strip is laid about four inches (ten centimetres) from the base of the headrest. It is folded over at the end for about one inch (two centimetres), cut edge uppermost, and then tacked into position with $\frac{5}{8}$ inch (15 millimetre) tacks, three along the outer edge of the rail and two towards the inner edge of the rail to make a W shape. Now the webbing is pulled, using a stretcher, towards the front rail where it is tacked through the single thickness

with three tacks, folded over for one inch (two centimetres) and tacked with two tacks. Another length of webbing is positioned in the same way about one inch to the right of the first length, to form a double tier. The next tier or twin set is placed about four inches (ten centimetres) along the right of the rail. Continue this way all along the frame towards the foot of the chaise-longue.

The same procedure is followed for the long lengths of webbing from the base of the head rail to the foot rail. These are also placed in pairs interlacing with the first strands.

The springs should be sewn to the webbing before they are lashed. To do this the frame is turned the right way up. The springs are placed on the webbing at the junction of the interweave. The ends of the springs, where the wire twists are rounded, are turned towards the middle of the seat. This means that when the springs are lashed they will form a dome shape in the centre of the seat, which is where most of the weight has to be taken.

Using a curved needle and a very long length of twine, penetrate the webbing from underneath, holding the spring with the other hand. The needle should come up just outside of the spring to catch the bottom ring of the spring when it is pushed downwards. The twine is then knotted to its own end. Make three stitches all around the base of the spring, tying a knot on the underside at each stitch. Do this for all the springs. The

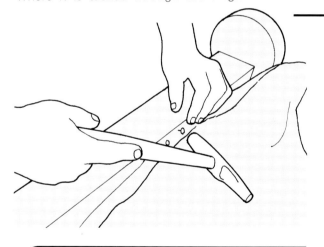

Stitching the bridle ties into the headrest is done in the same way as the bridle ties in the seat. Note that a curved needle is used because any other kind of needle would stick into the wood of the frame.

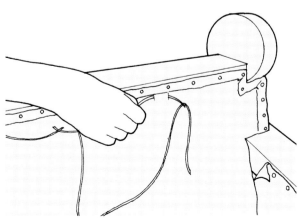

The next step is to fix the cloth to the headrest. Fold the allowance over, temporary tack it and finally fix it in the same way as for the seat. The hessian (burlap) should also be tacked along the sides and the bottom of the headrest and back. Leave the edge between the headrest and the back untacked so the subsequent layers of material can be pulled through to the frame.

Bridle ties for the top of the headrest and the back are placed by tying the twine around tacks which are spaced about six inches (15 centimetres) apart and not hammered home. The twine is tied under the head of the tack and then passed across the back of the hand to the next tack, allowing enough space for the stuffing. Then the tacks are hammered home.

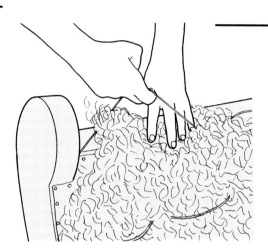

Place the horsehair in the bridle ties to a depth of about four inches (ten centimetres). First tease out the stuffing to remove any lumps. When the hair has been positioned in the bridles, insert more stuffing, especially in the middle of the seat to give a slightly domed effect.

twine should not be cut as you move from spring to spring. When the last spring has been stitched, tie the end of the twine to the main length in a slip knot and snip with scissors.

Lashing helps to secure the springs at the top so that they do not move about in the seat after a period of use. It also adds to the shape and finished appearance of the upholstery. A number of $\frac{5}{8}$ inch (15 millimetre) improved tacks (these are tacks with wide flat heads) is placed at the end of each row of springs on the frame and hammered to half their depth. The end of a length of laid cord (leaving a long tail) is then tied to one of the tacks and the tack is hammered to its full depth. The main length of cord is then tied in a half hitch round the second from top coil of the nearest spring, taken through the spring and tied round the top coil. The cord is then passed to the top coil of the next spring in the row, working from the back of the chair to the front, and tied in a half hitch round the top coil on the nearest side. The cord is again passed through the spring and tied to the opposite side. Continue to the top coil of the next spring, through to the second from top coil and secure the cord to the tack on the front rail which should then be hammered to its full depth.

There should then be a tail of cord at each tack long enough to reach back to the top coil of the nearest spring. This needs to be tied to the outside of the spring by pulling it so that the spring leans

outwards. Repeat this on all rows of springs. The test as to whether this has been done properly is that when the centre springs are depressed, the side springs should be upright. The next step is to attach hessian or burlap to all parts of the frame, with separate pieces for the headrest piece, seat and back. The material is cut with a one inch (two centimetre) allowance all round. This allowance is folded over and placed along the front or top rail with the cut edge uppermost. It is then temporary tacked into position at one inch (two centimetre) intervals and about half an inch (one centimetre) from the edge of the rail. It is smoothed over the surface and temporary tacked through a single thickness onto the rail at the base of the back, keeping the grain as straight as possible. The tacks are hammered to their full depth when the material is straight. Any excess material is turned back and then trimmed off.

The springs are attached to the hessian by the same stitch as that used to attach the springs to the webbing. Bridle ties, to hold the horsehair stuffing are then made in the material. Thread an upholsterer's needle with enough twine to go approximately twice around the area to be sewn. Start with a stitch in the hessian (burlap) one inch (two centimetres) long and one inch from the edge. Pull it through, leaving a four inch (ten centimetre) tail. Tie this tail to the main length of twine with a slip knot. Insert the needle into the hessian about four inches (ten centimetres) away, pointing it

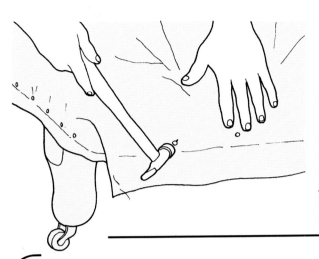

Now tack the scrim over the seat allowing the stuffing to overhang the edges of the seat by the same amount all around. Panel stitch the centre of the seat as described in the text. If the seat needs more stuffing, remove the temporary tacks at this stage and put in more horsehair. Then proceed with the tacking as in the project on the upholstered chair on page 61.

Extra stuffing should also be added around the edge of the scroll to give it more definition. When tacking the scrim over the scroll, it should be pleated round the scroll with tacks spaced at half inch (one centimetre) intervals. The tacks should be hammered into the chamfered edge, checking that the horsehair is still well edged before you do this. In this chaise-longue a line of tacks was driven through all layers into the front of the headrest rail to give the scroll further definition.

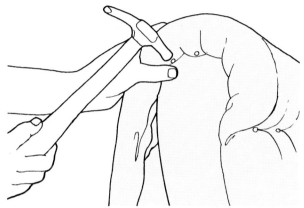

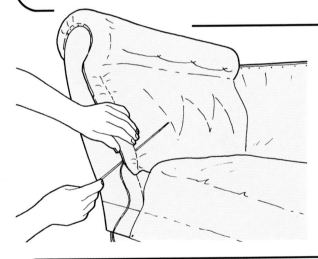

Top stitching forms an edge for the stuffing which has been drawn to the sides by blind stitching. This is done at all edges. The roll should be kept firm and evenly stuffed as you work.

When blind stitching along the length of the back, use stitches of half the normal size to prevent drag marks appearing in the scrim. This could be discernable when the top layer of fabric is in place.

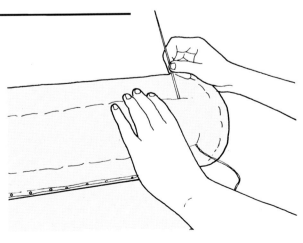

Next put a thin layer of horsehair stuffing in the depressions made by the top stitching. This is merely a skimming layer to even out the surface. Before covering the chaise-longue headrest with calico, sew a piece of tape along the calico where the headrest needs more definition in the front. Now pleat the calico cover in place around the scroll using special round headed pins. A pin should be placed in each pleat and then the calico stitched in place.

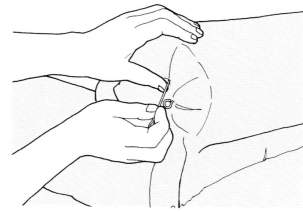

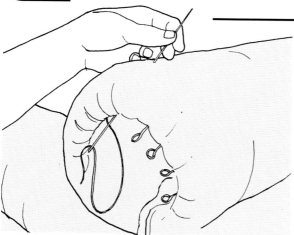

Stitch the pleats in the scroll with long stitches which should be triangular in shape. Put the needle into the pleat and bring it out in the scroll. Put the blunt end of the needle back into the scroll taking only a tiny stitch but bring the needle out about one inch (two centimetres) further down into another pleat on the scroll.

The calico should be temporarily tacked to the top rail of the back. It is then smoothed out and the tacks are driven home. Remember that the calico should be pulled tightly over the rolled edges with the grain straight. The tape sewn on the front will give definition to the front of the scroll. The wadding should then be placed over the whole piece to prevent the horsehair from coming through.

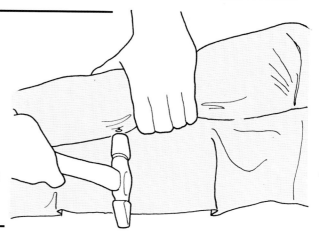

back towards the slip stitch. Pull the needle out about three inches (seven centimetres) from where you started. This will resemble a giant backstitch.

Bridle ties for the top rail of the headrest are placed by tying twine around the tacks which are spaced about six inches (15 centimetres) apart. The twine is tied under the head of each tack. Make sure that the bridles are loose enough for the stuffing by passing the twine over the flat of the hand. The horsehair is placed under the bridles and teased out to a depth of about four inches (ten centimetres). An extra layer of stuffing is placed under the scroll.

A piece of scrim with a one inch (two centi-

metre) allowance is used to cover the stuffing. It is placed centrally over the stuffing and temporary tacked at six inch (15 centimetre) intervals. The headrest and the back require separate pieces.

Using a long upholsterer's needle, the scrim is attached to the hessian or burlap about four inches (ten centimetres) from the edge of the seat, back and headrest. This stitch is called panel stitching and can either be triangular or rectangular in shape. Its purpose is to secure the stuffing in the centre of the piece. The needle is inserted through the scrim and stuffing and pushed out through the material at the bottom. The unthreaded end of the needle is pushed back through the stuffing and scrim to come up about half an inch (one centi-

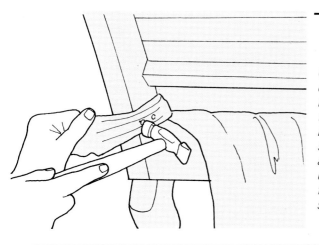

Cut out the furnishing fabric using the old cover as a pattern with plenty of extra all round to give ease with handling and tacking. When covering the headrest and back, pull the fabric tightly through the space between the back and the headrest and then tack it against the inside of the upright rail. You will need to slash the fabric at the uprights so take care at this stage.

To complete the covering of the scroll, make a template for the facing section. Check it for size against the chaise-longue before cutting out the furnishing fabric. Remember to leave enough fabric for turnings. Cut out a piece of wadding to the same pattern. Place the fabric and wadding in position with pins or skewers, turning under as you go.

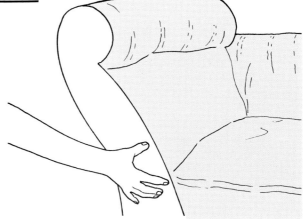

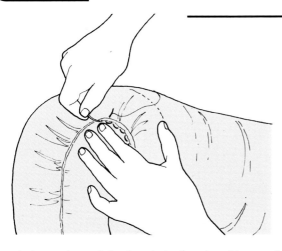

Before you slip stitch the facing in place, stand back from the piece and check that the pleats are tight and at regular intervals, about every half inch (one centimetre). Use a curved upholsterer's needle and a high quality thread. Select and apply an adhesive backed braid for the bottom edges. Tack a piece of black linen on the underside of the seat to act as a dust cover.

metre) from the original point of entry. The end is then tied to the main length in a slip knot. The needle is again pushed through the scrim four inches (ten centimetres) from the first stitch and brought through as before. The twine needs to be pulled tightly so that the scrim is forced down and the stuffing secured.

The temporary tacks are then removed and the scrim lifted so that more stuffing can be added at the edges to form a fat roll ready for blind stitching and top stitching. Pleat the scrim round the scroll with tacks placed about half an inch (one centimetre) apart. More horsehair can be added to the edges of the scroll to achieve a good fat edge. Tuck the scrim under the horsehair and tack down

to the frame along the edge of the wood.

The work thus far is then blind stitched by inserting the unthreaded end of the needle into the edges of the scrim at an angle of 45°. When blind stitching along the length of the scroll or other curved surfaces, use stitches of half the normal size to prevent drag marks from appearing on the scrim.

Top stitching forms an edge where blind stitching gathers the stuffing to the edge. Use a special tool called a regulator to keep the hair in the roll firm, thick and even, particularly at the corners. This tool can be improvised by using an upholsterer's needle and inserting it into the roll to re-position the horsehair.

Project 6

After the top stitching, a second layer of stuffing is used to fill the cavities made by the rolls of top stitching. This is then covered with calico which is tacked to the underneath of the rails at the back. The calico cover has to be pleated round the scroll. Place the pins or scewers in each pleat to keep the material firm as you stitch it permanently into place. The calico is then back stitched to the roll of the scroll from under and behind the edge.

The next step is to cover the calico with wadding to prevent the horsehair from protruding through the top cover. Remember that the calico should be pulled tightly over the rolled edges of the chaise-longue.

In this particular chaise-longue the scroll has an added feature of some definition on the front of the headrest as well as at the back. To give this line, drive a series of tacks through all layers into the front of the head rest rail. This should be done after the scrim has been tacked into place. Before you put the layer of calico over the final layer of stuffing, sew a strip of tape on the calico so that when it is placed in position and tacked over the scroll, the tape will lie along the line made by the tacks. The scroll will then be well enough defined so that the final furnishing fabric need only be pulled tightly over it and tacked to the carcass to give the desired effect.

To determine how much fabric you will need for the top cover, measure the old cover and allow at least six inches (15 centimetres) all round for fitting and ease of handling. Remember to make allowances if you are using a fabric with a nap or a pattern. The cover for the headrest and back should be pulled tightly through the space between the back and the headrest and tacked along the inside of the upright rail where it will be hidden.

To cover the scroll, a special template is made for the facing section. The material is then cut out and slip stitched in place over a piece of wadding to cover the wooden frame and give a soft line. Do not forget to cut templates for the other facing sections at the back of the headrest and at the end of the long back section. These should be cut, backed with wadding and stitched as for the front scroll facing.

The back of the headrest and the back should also be covered with fabric cut on the straight grain and these are slip stitched in place to cover the raw edges and the tacks. Finally the bottom of the chaise-longue is covered with a piece of black hessian or linen for a dust cover. This is known as bottoming.

The final step is to apply the braid. Most braids can be bought with a latex adhesive backing. However if the braid you want is not backed with adhesive, it is quite a simple matter to sew it in place all round the base (as in the colour picture on the right) with a slip stitch. During this final process of covering the chaise-longue with furnishing fabric, stand back from the work and check that it looks right, particularly the pleating over scrolls and on corners.

Below: The newly re-upholstered chaise-longue demonstrates that out of calamity an attractive piece of furniture can be given a new lease of life and provide a beautiful addition to any home

Project 7: A Writing Box

This ambitious project involves the restoration of a seemingly irreparable writing box. New materials such as leather and gold leaf are introduced, the inside section is rebuilt, and damaged inlay and veneer work are repaired

Left: The writing box needs a great amount of work to bring it back to its former glory. Half of the writing section is missing, the hinges to the existing part are broken, many of the inlays and veneers require replacing, the mother of pearl escutcheon has been removed from the lock, new dividers are needed in the top, and the leatherwork has to be replaced

At first sight this walnut writing box seems beyond the capabilities of most amateurs as a restoration job. Yet if you have tackled a number of projects and have proved to yourself that you have reached a reasonable level of proficiency, there is no reason why you should not go ahead and try. The skills needed are no more difficult than those required for the previous six projects. The only difference is that you will need to work with small pieces of veneer so that your touch must be sure and confident.

There is one important consideration though, if you have seen a similar box and are trying to decide whether to buy it and attempt to restore it, remember that some of the materials used, such as gold leaf, hide leather and, above all, mother of pearl, are expensive. There are a number of other materials which you can use as substitutes. By doing this, you could attempt the repairs described on the next few pages and gain valuable experience and learn from your mistakes with no great expense.

The box is in a sad state before restoration. The inside of the writing section is missing, the mother of pearl escutcheon (the cover for the keyhole) is almost all gone, some of the inlays are broken, the inside fittings or dividers need attention and replacement, the hinges for the writing section are missing and the lock and key need to be put into working order. Added to this, the leather on the writing section was severed when the inside section came away. Also, the main panel of the writing section has suffered from shrinkage and this is the task which should be tackled first.

The writing section is comprised of a main panel with its grain running horizontally and outside panels with the grain running vertically. Some form of excessive heat has caused the centre panel to shrink so that one of the side panels protrudes by a very tiny amount. In most cases this type of fault results in damage or stress marks in the veneer where the two panels have been joined. In more severe cases the joint actually opens so that the veneers are broken. This damage often takes years to become apparent. As the veneer usually gives a writing box its special character, you will be anxious to repair any cracks.

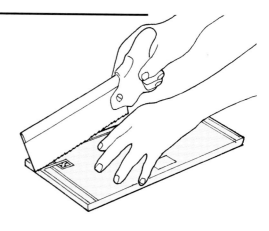

The lid has become distorted through shrinkage. To correct this, cut the corner to the joint of the inlay. This cut should be enough to reduce the side panel by the smallest fraction so that it can be refitted to correct the distortion. Now drill the piece and fit wooden pins. These are then glued into place. Any missing veneers and inlays should be replaced at this stage.

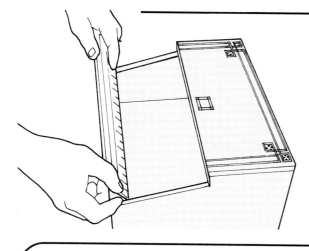

The missing section on the writing box is the lid that fits into the interior of the box. It should be cut from matching wood. To find the dimensions, first measure across the bottom, where the hinges are to be placed, across the top and then along both sides. The measurements are taken from the inside edges in all cases.

The new section of the lid is then veneered with matching veneers. These should be cut with a sharp knife and then glued into position. Press them down with a warmed hammer to squeeze out excess glue and to ensure a close fit. Make the veneer up to match those on the outside existing section of the lid.

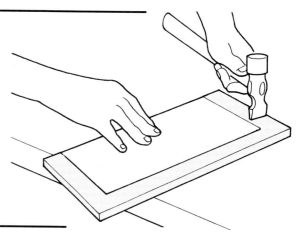

Left: A close-up of the beautiful but complicated inlays and veneers which are the chief feature of the box. Even in this small section the damage is extensive

The veneer and inlays on this writing box have not cracked under the strain of the shrinking so that it is possible to repair it. In many instances it is unwise to even consider tackling such a problem as the cure can often look a lot worse than the fault.

On this writing box the veneer has curved up at the joint. To repair it, it is necessary to cut into the joint of the inlay and then at right angles to the edge of the writing box. This will mean that you can remove the entire corner section. Be careful to cut along the line of the design so that when the piece is refitted, the design will still look the same as that on the other undamaged corner of the writing box. The wastage caused by the saw cut is sufficient so that when the same piece is refitted, it is flush with the main panel. To do this, drill into the sawn piece and into the centre panel and then glue and pin it back into position. Then make up the missing veneers and inlays using the methods described in the previous projects.

If you are presented with a similar problem where the shrinkage is very acute, you may have to think of an alternative way of dealing with it. If there is a clearly defined crack you may be able to insert a sliver of veneer over the crack in the surface wood but it is unlikely that you will be able to get a good enough finish and the repair will probably be noticeable. The most likely result of such stress is that stretch marks show on the surface of the veneers. One way of tackling this

Below: A view of the box showing that some of the dividers in the top section need replacing and giving a clearer view of the part of the writing section still intact, apart from torn leather

is by levelling these marks with wax coloured with a matching stain. Again the finish is unlikely to be completely satisfactory.

After dealing with the existing part of the writing section, the absent half needs to be replaced. This is the piece which settles into the interior of the box so that when the lid is opened it provides a writing surface covered in decorated leather. The dimensions need to be measured, making allowance for the veneer, and the replacement cut from a matching piece of wood. When the new section is made up and the veneers glued and pressed into place, the position of the hinges has to be determined and the holes drilled for the screws. Then renew the hinges as near to the originals as you can find. The new interior section is then laid in position and hinged to the existing writing section using a strip of canvas.

Canvas provides a good, strong joint and is often used in furniture restoration. The bottoms of drawers or chairs, for example, can be greatly strengthened using this form of joint. The canvas can be applied with a wallpaper paste mixed with water to up to three times its usual strength. There are a number of fish and vegetable glues now available which can also be used but these are relatively expensive. The wallpaper paste must be very thick or the water will penetrate and take a long time to dry. A really excessive amount of water will tend to weaken the canvas.

The next task on the writing box is to insert new dividers in the top of the box, the section for holding pens, pencils and ink bottles. Some of these were missing when the box was purchased. They are replaced using matching mahogany which is polished to colour before being fitted into the same grooves.

Mother of pearl is difficult and expensive to obtain. Ivory, tortoiseshell and even a hardwood can be used as an alternative, although ivory will not be any cheaper. Mother of pearl, ivory and tortoiseshell can be cut with a small hacksaw fitted with a fine blade. They can be glued into place with any animal glue. To make the glue extra effective, add a tiny piece of garlic.

The mother of pearl is then slotted into the escutcheon space and fitted before being glued. As for the lock and key, on this box, the key fitted so there is no problem. The lock works smoothly and there is practically no damage. If you are not so lucky with a similar box there are a number of ways of dealing with this problem. These are described in the chest of drawers project, and since this type of lock is relatively common you should have little difficulty in buying and fitting a replacement.

Before the next major task of applying the leather top to the writing section, the surface of the whole box should be cut down with fine steel wool. It is then revived and repolished, colouring all new pieces with a matching stain.

Before laying the new leather, all of the old

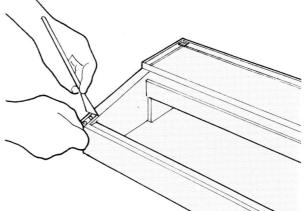

After removing the broken sections of the hinges, mark the wood for new hinges. Now hang the old part of the lid in place after first removing the worn piece of leather.

The new section of the lid (the writing section), complete with new veneers, should then be fitted into place with a special canvas hinge which is laid in a strip across both parts of the lid. This can also be made of strong linen.

Left: Inserting the mahogany dividers, these must first be coloured before being set in place

Below: The renovated writing section with a new canvas hinge, and the metal hinges set in place

Right: Carefully working the mother of pearl into the escutcheon with a pair of tweezers

leather should be stripped off and the surface prepared by sanding with one of the coarser grades of sandpaper to remove all traces of old glue. The whole area to be covered is usually enclosed with a veneer border. The commonly used leathers are light hide, morocco or skivver. A form of synthetic or imitation leather can also be used by those who do not mind using modern materials. Many of these imitations are of first class quality and are generally cheaper.

The tools needed for leather work and gilding include a tooling wheel with a plain line or decorative border, a sharp knife and a brush for spreading adhesive. Again, wallpaper paste should be used but diluted with only a third of the water suggested in the instructions. You will also need methylated spirit and a piece of cloth for wiping it over the wheel to clean it after it has been heated.

The leather should be cut tight into the veneer recesses to ensure a good fit. It is generally best to make the final cuts when the glue is almost dry. When applying the leather over the wet glue you will find that a certain amount of stretching will take place but this will be balanced out as the glue dries and the leather shrinks back to its original dimensions. Hold the knife flat against the veneer borders as you cut to avoid undercutting. Press the edges of the cut leather down with your thumbnail or with a piece of rounded wood. Do this carefully. Impressions are easily made but harder to get rid of.

If you do not wish to buy gold leaf you can tool the leather with just the impression made by the wheel. The wheel should be heated and cleaned with the cloth and methylated spirit. It is then applied to the leather with enough pressure to make an indentation. Continue round the area you have decided to tool.

Gold leaf can be bought as tape with a thin paper backing and this is the simplest form in which to use it. The leaf is laid along the border and the heated wheel is passed over it. The wheel should again be cleaned and the paper backing removed from the leaf. It is advisable to mark out the border very lightly, or at least the corners of the border. A straight edge can be used if you do not wish to mark the leather. A straight edge is best for just one border. For two borders it is advisable for the inexperienced to lay down some kind of marking to guide them as they work. The leather should not be tooled or the leaf applied until you are absolutely certain that the glue used to position the leather has thoroughly dried.

When the tooling is completed, repolish the box and apply a coat of wax for protection and to bring out the colour even more effectively. If faced with a similar restoration project you will find that the more esoteric aspects such as tooling or making the escutcheon are not as difficult as dealing with the veneers. These are hard to work accurately and you may also find it difficult to match the grain of those veneers which are still in position. It is sometimes useful to draw these grains onto a piece of tracing paper, leaving an empty space where the new piece will fit. This will enable you to lay the paper against pieces of veneer to find the best possible match after a process of trial and error.

When you have found the best possible match, glue the paper onto the veneer and cut round it with a fine fretsaw. Overcut by about an eighth of an inch (three millimetres). You will find that the paper makes the veneer easier to handle by preventing it from cracking or splitting.

Cut the veneer further with a straight edge and sharp knife before glueing it into position. If you find that the veneer tends to lift as the glue dries, you should clamp it with a C or G clamp, placing a

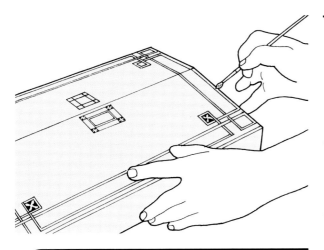

The next part of the restoration, after the glue on the canvas hinge has been allowed to dry, is to touch in the colouring to the new sections of veneer. This is done with a small artist's brush, using the tip only and laying the colour in confined sections so that it does not spill onto other parts of the box.

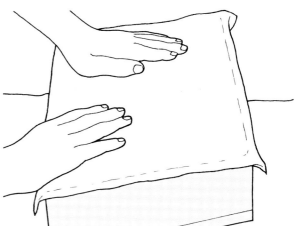

The bottom of the writing desk is covered with a baize protection. Glue this into position and firm it down with both hands. Wipe any excess glue away with a cloth and allow it to dry overnight.

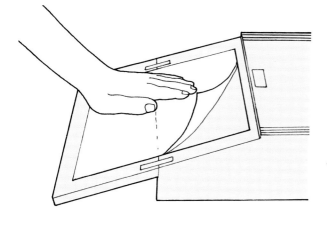

The leather should then be glued into position. Allow an excess at the edges so that it can be cut with a sharp knife to ensure not only a tighter fit but also a more accurate and professional finish. For the unsure hand, a straight edge such as a ruler should be used to guide the knife otherwise the edge of the leather will be jagged and the restoration will be spoiled. Great care should be taken so that the straight edge is placed along the right line and no unsightly gaps occur.

To lay the gold decoration on the leather, it is necessary to use a special rolling tool which consists of a wheel which has a design for decorative work or, if desired, just a plain border pattern. The wheel is first heated, after the borders have been very lightly marked, and the gold leaf, in tape form, is firmly impressed onto the leather. This tool is very expensive, as is the gold leaf, so many amateurs may find it more convenient to go to a leather shop and buy the leather complete with gold decoration.

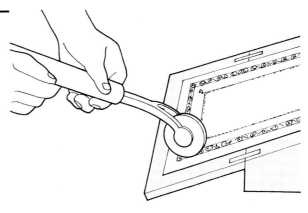

Right: The finished box with the gold leaf borders of the writing section in full view, contrasting with the beautiful veneers of the top

warmed piece of wood under the sole to protect the veneer.

The replacement of inlays is extremely difficult. Many of these bandings are no longer made for commercial use so that you could be faced with the daunting prospect of having to make them yourself. If only small pieces are needed it is not worth the effort and the inlays can be replaced with the thicker varieties of veneer.

An inlay is essentially a core of wood built up of pieces placed end to end so that their grains run in different directions. This core is glued together and then two pieces of veneer are glued to each side. The whole section is clamped while the glue is drying. Thin slices are then cut from this block to make the type of inlays shown on the lid of this writing box.

Another type of inlay used in walnut furniture is made on the same principle. Strips are cut across a block of wood at an angle of 45 degrees. These are glued together in two lengths and sandwiched between two pieces of veneer, usually ebony. Again, very thin strips are sliced to use as inlays.

If you use new veneers you will have to colour them with a small artist's brush. You should always test the colours first on a disposable piece of wood to avoid messing up the antique you are working on. You will probably find that a great deal of trial and error is necessary before you achieve the best approximate match. This may mean mixing different colours and even adding pigments to take the dullness from the colour.

The bottom of the writing box should also be covered for the protection of the surfaces on which it is to be placed. The best cover is a good quality baize. This should be cut and glued into place with a thick solution of wallpaper paste and after it has thoroughly dried, neaten the edges of the baize with a medium grade of sandpaper. When working with the paper always sand away from the baize toward the wood of the box.

The work required on the writing box will give you some idea of what to expect when tackling the rarer type of restoration. If you are a beginner to this type of woodwork you should tread carefully unless you have a lot of money to indulge a thoroughly enjoyable hobby.

Glossary

Applied Moulding Decorative moulding which is glued onto surfaces such as drawer fronts, doors and cabinet fronts.

Batten An end piece of narrow waste wood, which can be up to about 30 inches (75 centimetres) in length, it is used for clamping.

Bevelled Sloping edge cut in timber. The sloping edge of a chisel, for example, is bevelled.

Blind Stitching A series of stitches around the edge of the piece to pull the stuffing to the edge.

Blister A small section of veneer which has lifted because of lost adhesion.

Bracket Foot A short foot that forms an extension of the plinth member on a chest of drawers. It can be plain or rectangular, and may be carved or shaped in a number of ways.

Bradawl Like a gimlet, the bradawl is a tool which makes holes for starting screws. Bradawls have either square or tapered points.

Bridle Ties Long loose stiches sewn on the fabric under which the stuffing is positioned and partially held in place.

Carcass The main structure of a piece of furniture, excluding such parts as drawers, mouldings or feet.

Cocked Beads Decorative beads which are placed above the main surface of drawers and doors.

Cross Banding A slice or band of wood used as inlays or mouldings and consisting of a solid core of cross-grained blocks flanked by two sheets of veneer. Only used with certain types of furniture, such as that made from walnut.

Dovetail A joint made by a piece of wood lapped in series which receives the similarly shaped tails made in the wood to be joined.

Dowel A small, rounded piece of wood, usually made of birch, used for making or strengthening joints.

Flush When two adjacent surfaces are level, they are said to be flush.

Glazing Bar The framework used as a glazing foundation and moulding core on glass cabinet doors.

Glue Blocks A triangular block of wood where the two adjacent faces are at 90° and the pointed ends are squared off. Glue blocks are usually about two inches (five centimetres) long but can be longer for chairs. Used to strengthen jointed rails.

Knuckle Joint The revolving wooden joint used for swinging the flap leaves on gate-leg tables.

Loose Tenon A tenon inserted into a mortise which has its underside opened by cutting with a saw. Also a separate tenon glued into an open mortise or notch.

Mitre A piece of wood which has had its end cut at an angle of 45° is said to be mitred. Used for jointed picture frames.

Panel Stitching This holds the centre of a seat firm and attaches the scrim to the hessian through one layer of stuffing.

Plinth The base, usually separate, of cupboards, cabinets and desks.

Plugging Filling old screw holes with small, shaped wooden plugs.

Reviving Cleaning and renewing the polished surface of furniture.

Rubbed Joint A glued joint where no clamping is needed. Surfaces are planed flat and rubbed together slowly and gently until surplus glue is expelled and a kind of vacuum adhesiion is felt.

Rule Joint A hinged joint used on the leaves of gate-leg tables.

Stub Tenon A mortise and short tenon joint where the tenon cannot be seen once it is glued into place.

Stuck Moulding A moulding which has been cut from the solid carcass.

Top Stitching This forms the hard, firm edge after blind stitching has gathered the stuffing to the edge.

Turning A method of carving legs or arms of chairs and tables by means of a revolving lathe.

Veneer A thin layer of wood, noted for its grain and colour, used to decorate the showing surfaces of most kinds of furniture.

Windsor Chair A comfortable type of English country-made chair, usually executed in oak or beech, generally with arms and an arched back with numerous spindles. They were popular from the eighteenth century in America.

Further Reading

BEEDELL, S. *Restoring Junk* (Macdonald, London 1970; David Mackay, New York 1971)

Cane and Rush Seating (Larousse, New York 1976)

GLOAG, J. (Ed) *A Short Dictionary of Furniture* (Allen & Unwin, London 1969)

A Handbook of Hardwoods—Building Research Establishment (Her Majesty's Stationery Office, 1976)

A Handbook of Softwoods—Building Research Establishment (Her Majesty's Stationery Office, 1977)

HAYWARD, C. H. *Furniture Repairs* (Evans Brothers, London 1976; C. Scribner, New York 1976)

HAYWARD, C. H. *Practical Veneering* (Evans Brothers, London 1975)

HAYWARD, C. H. *Staining and Polishing* (Evans Brothers, London 1975; Drake, New York 1975)

HONOUR, H. *Cabinet Makers and Furniture Designers* (Weidenfeld & Nicolson, London 1969)

The International Book of Wood (Mitchell Beazley, London 1976; Simon & Schuster, New York 1976)

MacCARTHY, F. *All Things Bright and Beautiful. Design in Britain 1830 to Today* (Allen & Unwin, London 1972)

WATSON, F., *et al. The History of Furniture* (Orbis Publishing, London 1976; W. Morrow, New York 1976)

WINDRUM, F. *Converting Junk* (Macdonald, London 1974)

Guide to Materials and Suppliers in the U.K.

In the specialized area of furniture restoration, traditional materials may be difficult to obtain outside the trade and sometimes certain substances are sold only in bulk. With persistence, however, you should be able to find the precise product or a suitable alternative from the list of suppliers and manufacturers given here.

WOOD AND FITTINGS
To find the small amounts of wood needed to restore old furniture, scour the second-hand furniture shops or buy seasoned wood from timber merchants. Frequently, modern wood is not of the same quality as that used in the past, when it was often seasoned for more than 50 years before being used.

Veneers to match missing pieces are hard to find in shops and you will have to spend time looking for the better quality materials. Go to specialists in veneers, or lumber yards. Antique restorers may be prepared to sell you small amounts. One supplier of good-quality veneers to the public is **J. Crispin & Son**, 96 Curtain Road, London EC2.

Brass reproduction fittings are readily available from architectural ironmongers, cabinet brassfounders and locksmiths. If you have any difficulty, **J. D. Beardmore & Co Ltd**, 5 Percy Street, London W1 and **Shiner & Sons Ltd**, 8 Windmill Street, London W1, have large selections.

STRIPPING
Paint remover is available under many proprietary names in most DIY shops and ironmongers, such as Nitromors, made by **Wilcot (Parent Co.)**, Fishponds, Bristol, and Polystrippa by **Polycell Products Ltd**, Broadwater Road, Welwyn Garden City, Herts.

Caustic soda, available from most ironmongers and gardening shops, is the last resort in removing old polish. It should not be used on veneers as it will soften the glue.

Caustic soda darkens the wood. To bring it back to its original colour you can use a peroxide bleach. Peroxide No. 2 bleach is the best for pine. This is available from **Marrable & Co. Ltd**, Delamare Road, Cheshunt, Herts. To remove small stains, use an ordinary domestic chlorine bleach such as Superbleach, manufactured by **F. T. Morrell & Co**, 214 Acton Lane, London NW10.

If the stains persist, nitric or oxalic acid can be used diluted with two parts of water. These can be dangerous substances but they are available, often only in large quantities, from good ironmongers. Camphorated oil can be obtained from major chemists such as Boots.

There are many abrasives available and they come in different grades. Ask the sales assistant for advice on the best grade for your particular stripping job. The wet-and-dry carborundums are those impregnated with metal filings. Evostick Woodwork Adhesive, by **Evode Ltd**, Stafford, is an effective glue for all jobs.

Scratches and stains on light coloured furniture are dealt with by rubbing with sandpaper and applying linseed oil. This is readily available, but if you have any difficulty, **Rustins Ltd**, Drayton Works, Waterloo Road, London NW2 produces their own brand.

If woodworm has infected your furniture, treatment should be given before applying any finishing touches. **Rentokil Ltd**, 16 Dover Street, London W1 produces a woodworm fluid.

FINISHING
Before finishing the piece, you must make good the wood. This is done with a plastic wood filler paste. There are a number of proprietary brands — Brummer Stopping, manufactured by **Clam-Brummer**, Maxwell Road, Borehamwood, Herts, is particularly good and comes in many shades to match the existing wood. **Rustins Ltd**, Drayton Works, Waterloo Road, London NW2 produces one. There is a wax filler which looks a little like sealing wax and is used to fill cracks or knot holes. One brand is Stick Stopping and it is manufactured by **F. T. Morrell & Co.** 214 Acton Lane, London NW10.

After filling and staining, the wood can be coated with a shellac-based polish of which there are a great variety. One of the most popular is the French polish by **Rustins Ltd**, Drayton Works, Waterloo Road, London NW2.

A wax covering gives the final protective coating to the wood. Beeswax is the traditional one to use. It can be bought from good ironmongers such as **Barker & Sons Ltd**, 16 Queenstown Road, London SW8 or **Morrell's Stores**, 25 Beak Street, London W1, in block or flake form. If you cannot buy beeswax, then Antiquax, manufactured by **James Briggs & Sons Ltd**, Lion Works, Old Market Street, Blackley, Manchester 9, is a mixture of beeswax, carnauba wax and other waxes, and is easy to apply. Chilled wax is a brand of wax polish by **J. Nicholson & Sons Ltd**, 3 Bath Road, Leeds 11. It can be applied directly to bare wood.

UPHOLSTERY EQUIPMENT
The Russell Trading Co, 75 Paradise Street, Liverpool 1, and **Grant Baxell**, 195A Upper Richmond Road, London SW15 both have mail order catalogues with a full range of upholstery materials and tools. **Fred Aldous Ltd**, P.O. Box 135, 37 Lever Street, Manchester M60 1UX supplies cane by mail.

Index

Page numbers in italics indicate illustrations.